FRAMES AND MIRRORS

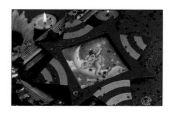

Creating a decorative frame to suit your picture or mirror is a truly satisfying craft. In this section you can find more than 20 fascinating frame projects in a wide range of materials and finishes. But frames do not have to be confined to a supporting role — these designs are eye-catching, decorative pieces in their own right. In addition to creative inspiration for new frames to make, this section offers ideas for revamping old frames and embellishing plain ready-made examples.

Just as important as a creative approach to making frames are fresh ideas as to what to display in them — as well as your favourite photos or prints, why not feature jewellery, textiles or even finds from the seashore or countryside?

MAKING MOUNTS (MATS)

Mounts (mats) and mounting

The mount is a cardboard window that is placed as a protection over the photograph or artwork to be framed. Take care to choose a colour that will set off the image.

MATERIALS AND EQUIPMENT
ruler
pencil
mountboard (mat board)
thick waste card
set square
metal rule (straight edge)
mount cutter
craft knife

Making mounts

Before framing a picture, first cut the mount (mat).

This usually has a bevelled or sloping edge, so that the eye is led into the picture. Wide margins look better in neutral colours.

Before you start it is a good idea to make a diagram of the mount showing its proportions and measurements so that you can refer to it while you are working. The area to be cut out must be at least 2.5 mm/⅛ smaller than the picture on each side.

Mark the measurement on the diagram, together with the measurements for top, bottom and sides, to calculate the overall size of mountboard (mat board) required.

1 Mark out the dimensions of the top, bottom, sides and sight area of the mount (mat) on the back of the mountboard (mat board). Place the board on a spare piece of thick waste card, not on a cutting mat.

2 Position the metal rule (straight edge) and cutter and slide the blade out just enough to cut the board. Move the blade, deepening the cut with each stroke. Overcut the corners slightly.

3 If the window does not fall away, use a craft knife to finish off the cut.

BELOW *Mountboards are available from most good stationery shops and come in a large range of proportions and colours.*

MATERIALS AND EQUIPMENT

Bevel edge mount cutter Hand-held tool for cutting bevelled edges in mountboard (mat board).

Bradawl Used to make guide holes for nails and screws.

Craft knife For general cutting and trimming. Always cut on a cutting mat and have spare blades to hand.

Cutting mat For cutting on when using a craft knife.

Frame clamp Adjustable clamp to hold glued frames together during drying.

Glass cutter For cutting glass.

Hacksaw For cutting hardboard.

Hand drill Useful for drilling small pins or nails into the frame to secure the moulding.

Masking tape Light sticking tape used for finishing off the back of a frame.

Metal carpenter's square For marking and cutting accurate right angles.

Metal rule To use as a guide when cutting straight lines with a craft knife or mount cutter.

Mitre saw Used for cutting moulding at accurate angles. The mitre saw shown has a range of pre-set angles and an integral saw.

Nail punch For recessing nails prior to filling.

Panel pins For pinning frames and fixing backing board in position.

Pencil For marking measurements on mounts (mats).

ABOVE *Equipment for making wood frames and surrounds.*

Picture wire Strong multi-stranded copper wire used for hanging frames.

Pliers For bending wire and removing old nails and panel pins.

Ruler For accurate measuring.

Screw eyes These are screwed into the back of the frame, and the picture wire is attached to them.

Tack hammer For hammering panel pins and nails.

Wire cutters Used to remove the heads from nails and for cutting picture wire to length.

Wood glue Strong adhesive for gluing mitre joints together.

PAPIER-MACHE MIRROR

This jolly papier-mâché herald is blowing a fanfare for your reflection – he's swapped his traditional banner for a miniature mirror. Paint his part-coloured costume in plenty of cheerful, bright shades to suit the mood of the piece.

YOU WILL NEED

MATERIALS
tracing paper
thin card
PVA (white) glue
newspaper
mirror, 5.5 cm/2¼ in square
white acrylic or matt emulsion (latex) paint
acrylic paints: red, purple, black, white, brown, green, permanent rose, blue, ivory and gold
gloss varnish
narrow red ribbon, 50 cm/½ yd
picture ring

EQUIPMENT
pencil
ruler
scissors
paintbrushes

1 Trace the template from the back of the book, enlarging it to 32 cm/12½ in high and cut it out of thin card. Using diluted PVA (white) glue, cover it with several layers of newspaper, building up the cheeks, nose, wavy hair and legs to create a relief effect. Allow to dry.

2 Cut two 6.5 cm/2½ in squares of card and glue the mirror in the centre of one. Cut out the centre of the second square, leaving a 1cm/ ½ in frame. Cover with newspaper strips. When dry, stick the frame to the mirror and backing, and build up with more layers of newspaper. Pierce two holes in the top of the frame.

3 Prime the herald and the mirror frame with white acrylic or emulsion (latex) paint. When this is dry, decorate with acrylic paints. When the paint is dry, protect with gloss varnish. With the ribbon, tie the mirror on to the trumpet. To complete, screw the picture ring into the back of the herald's shoulder.

SEASHELL MIRROR

This pretty mirror is decorated with paints and pieces of glass; it is created from moulded papier-mâché.

YOU WILL NEED

MATERIALS
tracing paper
strong card
paper pulp
newspaper
wallpaper paste
PVA (white) glue
white acrylic primer
glass "globs"
epoxy resin glue
gouache paints: deep yellow,
cadmium-yellow, deep cobalt,
pale blue, Cyprus-green,
grenadine, indigo and white
gold enamel paint
clear gloss varnish
mirror and fixing-tabs
plate-hanging fixture

EQUIPMENT
pencil
craft knife
cutting mat
small and fine paintbrushes
screwdriver

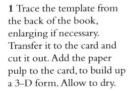

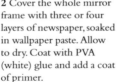

1 Trace the template from the back of the book, enlarging if necessary. Transfer it to the card and cut it out. Add the paper pulp to the card, to build up a 3-D form. Allow to dry.

2 Cover the whole mirror frame with three or four layers of newspaper, soaked in wallpaper paste. Allow to dry. Coat with PVA (white) glue and add a coat of primer.

3 When it is dry, attach the glass "globs" with epoxy resin glue. Decorate the frame with gouache paints, adding detail with the gold enamel paint.

4 Paint the frame with several coats of gloss varnish. Allow to dry. Secure the mirror with fixing-tabs. Attach the plate-hanging fixture, securing all screws with epoxy glue.

DRESSING TABLE MIRROR

This beautiful dressing-table mirror is made of papier-mâché pulp. Give free rein to your imagination and creativity by hand-painting it in the brightest and most beautiful colours.

YOU WILL NEED

MATERIALS
corrugated card
round mirror,
8 cm / 3 in diameter
epoxy resin glue
paper pulp
newspaper
wallpaper paste
PVA (white) glue
white acrylic primer
selection of gouache paints
clear gloss and clear matt
varnish
gold enamel paint

EQUIPMENT
pencil
craft knife
cutting mat
paintbrushes
paint-mixing container

1 Draw your chosen design on to the corrugated card. Cut it out carefully with a sharp craft knife using a cutting mat to protect the work surface.

2 Glue the mirror in position with epoxy resin glue.

3 Carefully build up paper pulp on the card all around the mirror. Do not place any pulp over the mirror, but ensure the pulp butts up to the edge. Dry thoroughly.

4 Apply several layers of newspaper dipped in wallpaper paste over the dried pulp, just overlapping the edges of the mirror. Allow to dry.

5 Coat with a layer of PVA (white) glue and then with some white acrylic primer. Allow the paint to dry between each stage.

6 When the paint is dry, cut away the excess paper that overlaps the edge of the mirror, to create a perfectly smooth finish.

7 Paint on your design in gouache paints; note that the back of the mirror is as important as the front.

8 When dry, coat in three or four layers of gloss varnish, adding matt varnish as a contrast in some areas. Allow to dry thoroughly between each stage. Finish with gold enamel detail.

GOTHIC STAR MIRROR

Use curly sausages of clay and cut out simple, freehand star shapes to decorate the frame of this mirror. To make sure the frame is symmetrical, fold a sheet of paper in half, draw a simple template and transfer it to the card before you cut.

YOU WILL NEED

MATERIALS
*thick card
mirror,
12.5 x 7.5 cm/5 x 3 in
masking tape
short length of thin wire
newspaper
PVA (white) glue
white emulsion (latex) paint
self-hardening clay
acrylic paints
varnish*

EQUIPMENT
*craft knife
cutting mat
paintbrushes
clay-modelling tools*

1 Draw the shape of the frame on to the card twice and cut it out. Cut out the central shape from the front piece of the frame. Fix the mirror to this piece with masking tape. Make a hook from wire and fix it to the back of the frame. Put the two pieces of card together, and tape securely.

2 Tear the newspaper into squares about 2.5 cm/1 in across and use PVA (white) glue to stick them in a single layer on both sides and around the edges of the frame. Allow to dry.

3 Prime with white emulsion (latex) paint and allow to dry. Roll some clay into long sausages and use to make an edging for the mirror, and decorative scrolls and curls. Press on to the frame. Cut star shapes out of the clay and fix on. Dry out. Decorate the frame with acrylic paints. Varnish when dry.

FOLK ART FRAMES

These simple, graphic frames combine the naïve, hand-painted feel and typical colours of folk art decoration with a boldness that makes them fit for the most sophisticated modern interior.

YOU WILL NEED

MATERIALS	EQUIPMENT
plain, flat-faced wooden frames	*fine-grade sandpaper cloth*
masking tape	*wide, flat-bristled and*
acrylic paints: white, yellow,	*fine paintbrushes*
black, raw umber, blue and red	*paint-mixing container*
tracing paper	*pencil*
satin polyurethane varnish	

1 Sand the frames to remove any lacquer and to provide a key for the paint. Wipe off any dust with a damp cloth. Mask off the corners of the frames diagonally with tape to prevent any brush marks from overlapping and lying in the wrong direction.

2 Mix up an "antique" yellow from white and yellow paint, with a touch of black and raw umber. Paint on the background colour on the top and bottom edges; this can be a single, quite thick coat, several coats, or a colour-wash, so that the wood grain shows through. Remove the tape when dry, mask the painted edges at the corners and paint the sides of the frames.

3 Trace the templates from the back of the book, enlarging them if necessary. Paint the templates to try out different colour combinations, if you like. Position the templates on the frames and draw around them with a soft pencil.

4 Paint the design directly on to the frames, adding the circle and star motifs. Varnish the frames to finish.

PICTURE FRAME

This project combines all the creative possibilities of stamping. It involves four processes: painting a background, stamping in one colour, over-printing in a second colour and rubbing back to the wood.

YOU WILL NEED

MATERIALS
picture frame
emulsion (latex) paints: sky-blue, red-brown and gold

EQUIPMENT
paintbrush
plate
foam roller
small and large star stamps
fine wire wool or sandpaper

1 Paint the frame sky-blue and leave it to dry.

2 Spread a small amount of red-brown paint on to a plate and run the roller through it until it is evenly coated. Ink the first stamp and print it in the middle of each side.

3 Using the red-brown paint, stamp a large star over each corner. Allow to dry.

4 Ink the large stamp with gold and over-print the red-brown corner stars. Allow to dry before rubbing the frame gently with fine wire wool or sandpaper. Experiment with dropped shadow effects and some other designs as well.

CRACKLE VARNISHED ANTIQUE

*By using antique varnish with a crackle varnish and
rubbing raw umber oil paint into the cracks, you can
give a frame a wonderful air of aged
and distinguished distinction.*

YOU WILL NEED

MATERIALS	EQUIPMENT
frame	*paintbrush*
wood filler and wood glue	*soft cloths*
(optional)	
white emulsion (latex) paint	
antique varnish	
crackle varnish	
raw umber oil paint	

1 If the frame is old, repair it with wood filler and glue. Prepare the frame with one or two coats of white emulsion (latex) paint.

2 Apply one coat of antique varnish to the frame. Allow to dry.

3 Apply a coat of crackle varnish to the frame. The cracks may take a long time to appear, depending on the humidity of the room. To speed up the process, you could carefully place the frame over a heat source for a few moments.

4 When the cracks appear, rub raw umber oil paint into them with a cloth. Allow to dry for 10 minutes. Apply a second coat of antique varnish to seal and protect the finish.

LEMON MIRROR FRAME

Hunt around for interesting printed material to combine with the lemon motif on this very striking papier-mâché frame. You could use a photocopier to reproduce graphics from books, or you could produce an ancient manuscript of your own choice.

YOU WILL NEED

MATERIALS
corrugated card
mirror, 15 x 18 cm/6 x 7 in
wallpaper paste
newspaper
acrylic paints: black,
yellow and green
paperclip
acrylic gesso
lemon motif wrapping paper
scraps of printed paper or
manuscript
white tissue paper
matt acrylic varnish

EQUIPMENT
craft knife
metal ruler
cutting mat
mixing bowl
paintbrush
natural sponge

1 Cut two 17 x 20 cm/6½ x 8 in rectangles, from the corrugated card. Lay the mirror centrally on one piece and cut strips of card to fit around it down two sides and across the bottom. Cut a window out of the centre of the other rectangle of card, leaving a 4 cm/1½ in border.

2 Coat the card with wallpaper paste and dry. Coat strips of newspaper with wallpaper paste and cover the front of the frame. Paste the spacer strips in position on the sides and bottom of the back panel, cover with papier-mâché strips. Dry, then apply a second layer.

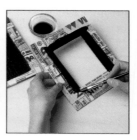

3 When the papier-mâché is dry, paint the inside surfaces of the frame black to minimize any possible reflection they might give in the mirror.

4 Open out the paperclip and thread one end through the papier-mâché at the centre back of the frame. Paste strips of newspaper over the clip, leaving the top section showing to act as a hook.

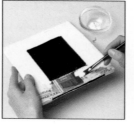

5 Join the front of the frame to the back with more strips of pasted newspaper. Paste folded strips over the top of the frame to either side of the opening for added strength. Once dry, paint the frame with acrylic gesso.

6 Sponge the entire frame with thin yellow paint, then with green paint to create an all-over mottled effect.

7 Tear the lemon motifs from the wrapping paper in interesting shapes and then arrange them over the frame. Fill the gaps between the lemons with small pieces of printed paper. Paste in position.

8 To soften the design, tear small pieces of white tissue paper and paste them on to the frame, crinkling them slightly and overlapping the edges of some of the motifs. When the paste is dry, paint the frame with two coats of matt acrylic varnish and insert the mirror into the top slit to finish.

CORONET PICTURE FRAME

*The coronet motif sets off
the regal gold and purple
of this frame.*

YOU WILL NEED

MATERIALS
*medium-density fibreboard
(MDF), 18 mm/¾ in
18 x 23 cm/7 x 9 in
polyester wadding (batting),
23 x 36 cm/9 x 14 in
crimson velvet,
45 x 45 cm/18 x 18 in
double-sided tape
50 cm/20 in gold braid,
2 cm/¾ in wide
50 cm/20 in gold cord
selection of large sequins or
filigree buttons
sewing thread
tracing paper
thin card or paper
sheet tin, 10 x 18 cm/4 x 7 in
glass gems
mountboard,
18 x 25.5 cm/7 x 10 in
white velvet,
5 x 15 cm/2 x 6 in*

EQUIPMENT
*dust mask
ruler
pencil
jigsaw
scissors
staple gun
needle
glue gun*

1 Wear a dust mask. Using a jigsaw, cut a 9 x 14 cm/3½ x 5½ in rectangle from the centre of the MDF to leave a frame measuring 4.5 cm/1¾ in deep. Cover the front with two layers of polyester wadding (batting) and snip out the area in the centre.

2 Cover the frame with a crimson velvet rectangle, 28 x 36 cm/11 x 14 in, fixing it tautly at the back with a staple gun. Make a slit in the centre and snip into the inner corners. Pull the inner edges of the velvet to the back of the frame. Staple.

3 Fix double-sided tape to the back of the gold braid. Remove the backing paper and stick around the inside edge of the frame to cover the raw edges. Stick a length of gold cord around the lower edge of the braid.

4 Sew sequins or filigree buttons to the four inside corners of the frame.

5 Trace the template from the back of the book, enlarging it to 15 cm/6 in across, and cut it out of thin card. Draw around it on sheet tin and cut out. Bend the side tabs inwards and curve the coronet gently. Decorate with glass gems stuck on with a glue gun.

6 Cut an oval shape from the remaining crimson velvet and sew a gathering thread around the edge. Crumple a sheet of paper and place in the centre, then draw up the thread. Fix inside the coronet with a glue gun.

7 Trim the top of the mountboard to fit the frame, leaving a wide tab to support the coronet. Tape the picture to be framed to the back of the opening, then using the staple gun staple the board to the back of the frame.

8 Use the glue gun to fix the coronet to the frame and board. Conceal the join by turning in the raw edges of the white velvet to make a narrow band and gluing it around the base of the coronet.

SUNNY DAISY FRAME

This vibrant painted frame with flowers of childlike simplicity is further enhanced by a charming pattern of gilded swirls.

YOU WILL NEED

MATERIALS
frame
acrylic gesso
acrylic paints: ultramarine,
cobalt-blue, titanium-white
and cadmium-yellow
satin varnish
3-hour oil size
Dutch gold leaf transfer book

EQUIPMENT
paintbrushes
paint-mixing container
coarse-grade sandpaper
soft cloth

1 Paint the frame with acrylic gesso in thin layers with a damp paintbrush. The gesso takes about 30 minutes to dry between coats. Apply at least four coats to form a solid base for the colour.

2 Mix some ultramarine and cobalt-blue paint and paint over the gesso base. Allow to dry, then rub over the frame to give a "sgraffito" look. Buff with a dry cloth; the gesso will dissolve if wet.

3 Paint four daisy flowers in the corners. Paint a design of stitches around the edge of the frame in white. Allow to dry. Give the frame a coat of satin varnish and allow to dry.

4 Gild the frame by painting 3-hour size swirls on to it. When the size is tacky, place the gold leaf transfer on top and rub gently with your finger. Dry for 24 hours.

DRIFTWOOD FRAME

This frame can be made from any beach finds. Wood that has been smoothed and weathered by the sea is best. Add shells or pebbles for variety. A seascape picture is ideal for a driftwood frame.

YOU WILL NEED

MATERIALS
flat-faced wooden frame
emulsion (latex) paints: deep and pale blue
wax furniture polish
selection of driftwood
strong glue
shells and beach finds
short piece of old rope
small toy boat

EQUIPMENT
paintbrushes
cloth
fine-grade sandpaper

1 Paint the wooden frame with a base coat of deep blue. Allow to dry, then rub on a layer of wax furniture polish and allow to dry.

2 Paint on two coats of pale blue, leaving to dry between coats. Sand away the top coat to reveal the base colour in places.

3 Arrange the driftwood pieces around the frame in a pleasing design. Glue in place. Add any shells and beach finds you have got.

4 Glue the old piece of rope on to the back of the frame to act as a hanging hook. Finally, glue the toy boat on to the top of the frame.

SEAHORSE FRAME

This frame-decorating idea would complement a picture with a seashore subject. It would be equally suited to a mirror, perhaps in a bathroom with a blue and white colour scheme. Shells are popular motifs for bathroom fabrics and wallpapers, and this frame would co-ordinate perfectly.

YOU WILL NEED

MATERIALS	EQUIPMENT
modelling clay	*rolling pin*
seashells and seahorse	*polythene sheet (optional)*
ready-made frame	*clay-modelling tools*
epoxy resin glue	*paint-mixing container*
acrylic paints: blue, white and	*small flat-bristled and*
lemon-yellow	*fine paintbrushes*
gold powder	
clear matt varnish	

1 Take a lump of clay and roll it into a ball. Roll the ball into a thick sheet. Press a shell into the clay, to create a negative impression. Repeat with the other shells and the seahorse. Allow to dry for several days.

2 Take another ball of clay and roll it out in the same way. Press it into the moulds, filling the shell and seahorse impressions. Carefully lift off the clay and place it face-up on the work surface.

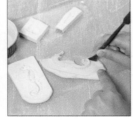

3 Cut away the excess clay from around each shape. Set aside and allow to dry for several days.

4 Arrange the shell and seashore shapes around the frame and glue them carefully in position.

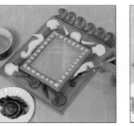

5 Mix the acrylic paints to make a turquoise colour. To achieve a slight verdigris effect do not mix the colours too thoroughly. Paint the shapes and allow to dry.

6 Mix the gold powder with varnish, varying the amount of varnish depending on the consistency you want to achieve. Highlight the shapes with gold.

GILDED FRAME

Transform a plain picture frame with gilded seashells, starfish and seaweed. This would be an ideal frame for a mirror – hang it up to allow the gilding to catch the light.

YOU WILL NEED

MATERIALS
flat-faced wooden frame
acrylic gesso
acrylic paints: titanium-white
and raw sienna
clear matt varnish
3-hour oil size
Dutch gold leaf transfer book

EQUIPMENT
decorator's and fine
paintbrushes
paint-mixing container
fine-grade sandpaper
soft pencil
sharp modelling tool

1 Paint the frame with acrylic gesso and allow to dry. Then make up a creamy wash from diluted white and raw sienna acrylic and paint the frame again. Allow to dry completely.

2 Lightly sand the frame to distress it slightly and let the wood grain show through. Apply three coats of varnish, allowing each to dry before applying the next.

3 Draw loose, freehand shell, seaweed and starfish shapes in pencil on the frame.

4 Paint size on to the shapes and, when they are tacky, gently press gold leaf on to the size. Brush off any excess. Scratch into the gilded surface with a modelling tool to give additional texture.

GOLDEN MIRROR

The contrasts of gold paint and metallic copper combine to flattering effect in this mirror frame. The curvaceous shapes in twisted wire set off the graphic copper triangles to create a stylish effect that will be at home in any contemporary décor.

YOU WILL NEED

MATERIALS

copper sheet
copper wire
modelling clay
small round mirror
terracotta acrylic paint
gold powder
matt varnish

EQUIPMENT

tin snips
ruler
wire-cutters
jeweller's pliers
rolling pin
clay-modelling tools
paint-mixing container
paintbrushes

1 Cut out six triangles from the copper sheet. Cut the wire into twelve 25 cm/10 in lengths. With the pliers, bend six wires into zigzags and six wires into spirals.

2 Roll the clay to 5 mm/¼ in thick. Cut two 13 cm/5 in circles. From the centre of one, cut a 6 cm/2½ in circle. Place the mirror in the centre of the other and the wires and triangles around the edge.

3 Place the second clay circle on top and smooth the edges together with a wet modelling tool. Allow to dry for several days.

4 Paint the clay with terracotta acrylic paint and allow to dry. Mix the gold powder with the varnish and paint a coat of the mixture over the terracotta.

SUNFLOWER MIRROR

You may not always feel cheerful when you look in the mirror, but this sunflower face is sure to lift your spirits. It could grace a dressing table or look good as a decorative object in any room in the house.

YOU WILL NEED

MATERIALS	EQUIPMENT
card	pair of compasses
modelling clay	pencil
small terracotta or plastic	ruler
flowerpot	scissors
8 mm/⅜ in diameter	rolling pin
plaster of Paris	plaster-mixing container
aluminium tubing,	clay-modelling tools
20 cm/8 in	old ballpoint pen
7 cm/2¾ in diameter mirror	paint-mixing container
acrylic paints: yellow, white,	paintbrush
chocolate-brown and green	

1 Cut out a circular card template of 12 cm/4¾ in diameter. Cut out a 6 cm/2½ in diameter circle from the centre of this circle. Roll out a sheet of clay to a thickness of 5 mm/¼ in and cut out two rings. Seal the drainage hole in the bottom of the flowerpot with clay.

2 Mix up the plaster and pour it into the pot. When the plaster is semi-dry, insert the tube in the middle. Allow to dry. Remove the tube. Place the mirror in the centre of one ring and place the tube with one end resting on the bottom edge of the circle. Put the second ring on top. Seal the edges with a wet modelling tool.

3 Roll out another sheet of clay 3 mm/⅛ in thick, in a long oval shape. Cut out regular flower petal shapes.

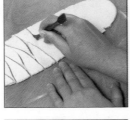

4 Attach petals all around the back of the mirror, sealing the edges with the tool. Then attach petals to the front, so that they cover the spaces between the back petals. Bend some of the flower petals to make the sunflower look realistic.

5 Roll two long thin clay "sausages" and put one on top of the join between the petals and the mirror and one at the mirror edge. Press the end of a pen into the "sausages" to create little depressions all over.

6 Mix the two yellow and white paints to make a bright, sunny yellow, then paint the sunflower petals yellow with it.

7 Paint the border around the mirror with chocolate-brown. Remove the tube and paint it green. Re-insert the tube in the flowerpot and fit the mirror on top.

FELT COLLAGE FRAME

Felt is a great material because it does not fray when cut and it can be either sewn or glued in place. It comes in vivid colours, so it is ideal for a bright, modern interior. Copy the fluid outline of the frame shown here or experiment with your own ideas.

YOU WILL NEED

MATERIALS	EQUIPMENT
medium-density	pencil
fibreboard (MDF)	dust mask
emulsion (latex) paint	jigsaw
selection of felt sheets	paintbrush
fabric glue	ballpoint pen
	scissors

1 Copy your chosen design on to MDF and, wearing a dust mask, cut out the frame with a jigsaw. Apply a coat of paint and allow to dry. Place the frame on a sheet of felt and draw around it.

2 Snip the centre diagonally and cut out the felt. Glue the piece of felt on to the front of the frame. Glue the centre flaps back over the rebate on to the back of the frame.

3 Cut out a zigzag felt border and stick it to the inner edge of the frame. Glue narrow strips of felt in a contrasting colour around the rebate of the frame.

4 Cut out the felt shapes for decoration and stick them all over the frame.

LEAFY FRAME

This picture frame has a very warm autumnal feel about it, and it really would make a nostalgic souvenir of a woodland walk in the beautiful countryside.

YOU WILL NEED

MATERIALS
*selection of leaves in various colours
paper towels
wooden frame with a wide, flat moulding
PVA (white) glue
crackle glaze
raw umber oil paint*

EQUIPMENT
*flower press or heavy book
paintbrush
soft cloth*

1 Make sure that all the leaves are thoroughly dry, and then place them between layers of paper towels in a flower press or between the pages of a heavy book. Leave for at least a week to dry completely.

2 Glue the leaves on to the frame, coating them one at a time and waiting for them to dry partly before sticking down. Begin by arranging a row of overlapping leaves around the outer edge of the frame.

3 Make a second round, using different leaf types. Select four large leaves for the corners. Fill gaps with smaller leaves. When the frame is covered, paint it with a layer of PVA (white) glue. Allow to dry.

4 Paint the frame with crackle glaze, following the manufacturer's instructions. When the cracks appear, rub some raw umber oil paint into the surface of the glaze with a soft cloth.

KING OF HEARTS MIRROR

This clay mirror frame is very easy to make, but it looks sophisticated. The heart-shaped cut-away section, outlined with glittering copper wire, makes a really unusual mirror that will be as welcome for its decorativeness as it is for its usefulness.

YOU WILL NEED

MATERIALS
copper wire
rectangular mirror
self-hardening clay
tracing paper
turquoise acrylic paint
gold powder
clear varnish

EQUIPMENT
wire-cutters
round-nosed pliers
polythene sheet
rolling pin
pencil
clay-modelling tools
small paintbrushes
paint-mixing container

1 Shape a length of wire into a heart with an internal curl to fit within the mirror.

2 Shape two lengths of wire into curls with a right angle at the other end.

3 Roll out the clay to a thickness of 4 mm/³⁄₁₆ in on polythene.

4 Trace the template from the back of the book and cut out a clay "crown" with a wet modelling tool. Cut out a clay rectangle at least 2 cm/¾ in larger than the size of the mirror.

5 Sandwich the mirror between the "crown" and the rectangle. Smooth the clay to get an impression of the mirror. Lift off the rectangle and cut 1 cm/½ in larger than the impression.

6 Replace on the mirror, matching the impression to the mirror outline. With a wet modelling tool, carefully seal the join between the two clay layers.

7 Place the wire heart on top and, with a wet modelling tool, cut around the inside of the heart, revealing the mirror. Carefully insert the wire curls on one side.

8 Mould clay into "buttons" to stick on to the mirror frame under the crown and allow to dry for several days.

9 Give the clay a coat of turquoise paint and allow to dry thoroughly.

10 With a dry brush, cover the frame lightly with gold powder. Finally, give the frame a coat of varnish.

WOODEN STAR FRAME

Make your favourite person an instant star by putting their picture in this original frame. Once the photograph is in position, back it with a piece of stiff card cut to size and held in place with tape.

MATERIALS	EQUIPMENT
picture or photograph	*ruler*
birch plywood sheet,	*pair of compasses*
5 mm/¼ in thick	*pencil*
white undercoat paint	*fretsaw*
acrylic paints	*sandpaper*
satin varnish	*router*
brass triangle picture hook	*paintbrushes*
and pins	*hammer*

1 Measure your picture and subtract 1 cm/½ in from each dimension to work out the size of the frame opening. Mark this on the plywood, then mark out the star pattern from the back of the book around it.

2 Cut out the star shape and inner square and sand down all the edges. On the back, rule a line around the opening 5 mm/¼ in from the edge and make a rebate with the router 3 mm/⅛ in deep. Sand the edges.

3 Paint the frame with white undercoat, sanding down lightly when dry. Apply another coat of paint. Mark out the bands in pencil, then paint the design.

4 Finish with a coat of satin varnish. Finally, pin a triangle hook to the top point of the frame.

PRIMITIVE FRAMES

Simple wooden frames can be transformed into a richly patterned, colour-matched set with acrylic paint and pre-cut rubber stamps. The three frames used here are all different, but they have enough in common to be treated as a group.

YOU WILL NEED

MATERIALS
*3 wooden frames
acrylic paints: sienna, sea-blue,
stone and maize-yellow
clear matt varnish (optional)*

EQUIPMENT
*fine-grade sandpaper
paintbrushes
3 plates
3 rubber stamps*

1 Follow the same procedure for all frames, using different colours and rubber stamps. Sand down and paint each frame. Allow to dry, then apply a second coat for a solid covering of colour.

2 Mix some sienna paint into the sea-blue to produce an olive-green colour. Spread an even coating of the other colours on to separate plates.

3 Dip a stamp into the paint to make a test print on scrap paper to ensure that the stamp is not overloaded with paint. Print closely-spaced motifs on to the background colour.

4 Stamp the design over every visible surface, going over the edges and around the sides. When the paint is dry, give each frame a coat of clear matt varnish, if you like.

BEADED VELVET FRAME

The luxurious texture and glowing colour of velvet is highlighted with the jewel-like colours of glass and metallic beads, to produce an effect of considerable sophistication and style.

YOU WILL NEED

MATERIALS	EQUIPMENT
card	pencil
velvet square	ruler
matching thread	craft knife
metallic beads	cutting mat
glass beads	sharp-pointed scissors
self-adhesive felt	needle
PVA (white) glue	dressmaker's pins

1 Cut out a square from the card at least 1 cm/½ in smaller than the velvet square. Cut out a square from the middle to make a frame. Place the velvet right-side down and put the frame on top. On the outside edge, leave a 1 cm/½ in seam allowance and mitre the corners. Cut away the middle section of velvet leaving a 1 cm/½ in seam allowance and snipping into the corners. Sew large stitches along the velvet and pull the sides together over the back of the frame.

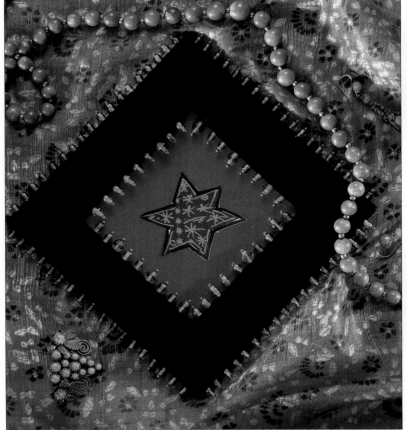

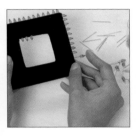

2 Thread the beads on to the pins, first a metallic and then a glass one on each pin. Push the beaded pins firmly into the inside and outside edges of the card.

3 Cut a backing square from the card at least 1 cm/½ in smaller than the finished frame. Cover it on both sides with felt. Glue it on the back of the frame on three sides.

PAW PRINT FRAME

Folk art frames were often made from common woods painted and grained to imitate something much grander, such as maple or walnut. The paw print in particular was a popular pattern in which the surface was covered with spots resembling different animal tracks.

YOU WILL NEED

MATERIALS
frame
emulsion (latex) paints:
red-ochre and
pumpkin-yellow
artist's acrylic or stencil
black paint
paper towels
clear water-based varnish
artist's acrylic paints: raw
and burnt sienna

EQUIPMENT
decorator's, stencil and
household paintbrushes
fine-grade steel wool

1 Paint the frame with a base coat of red-ochre, then allow to dry. Apply a coat of pumpkin-yellow.

2 Hold a brush with black paint in a vertical position and push down slightly while twisting it on the frame. Too much paint will "blob", so rub the brush on paper towels between dips.

3 When the paint is completely dry, rub the edges lightly with steel wool to simulate wear and tear.

4 Tint the clear varnish with a small amount of raw and burnt sienna and apply to the frame. Add a finishing coat of clear varnish.

PHOTOGRAPH FRAME

Because of its softness, fine-gauge aluminium foil is the perfect material for cladding frames. Coloured and clear glass nuggets combine with the subdued tones of the foil to give this frame a Celtic air, reinforced by a design of repeating circles, a fundamental element in Celtic decorative art.

YOU WILL NEED

MATERIALS
photograph frame
36 gauge/0.005 in
aluminium foil
epoxy resin glue
thin card
coloured and plain
glass nuggets

EQUIPMENT
ruler
scissors
pencil
ballpoint pen

1 Remove the glass and backing from the frame. Measure the four sides and cut strips of foil to cover them, making the foil long enough to wrap over and under, to the back. Mould the foil strips around the frame and glue in place.

2 Cut pieces of foil to cover the corners. Mould these to the contours of the frame and glue them in place.

3 Draw a circle on to card and cut out to make a template. Draw around the card on to the aluminium foil, using a ballpoint pen. Cut out the foil circles. Draw a design on to one side of each circle. This is now the back of the circle.

4 Turn the foil circles over so that the raised side of the embossing is face up. Glue coloured glass nuggets to the centre fronts of half of the foil circles. Glue plain glass nuggets to the centres of the other half.

5 Glue the foil circles around the photograph frame, spacing them evenly. Alternate the circles so that a coloured glass centre follows one with clear glass. When the glue is dry, replace the glass and backing in the frame.

HOME
ACCESSORIES

Surround yourself with beautifully hand-crafted objects and furniture from this section. Ideas range from lampshades to a bench and from storage tins to a child's chair. Many objects you already have in your home can be easily revamped and turned into works of art, rather than the utilitarian shop-bought products they may once have been.

Most of the projects here can be easily adapted to suit your existing decor and tastes – for example, just change the colours, or design a different motif. These projects are here to inspire you, to provide you with the basic techniques and to inform you about materials and equipment – the rest is up to your imagination.

GILDING

One of the simplest and most beautiful ways of decorating household ornaments is by gilding or applying other metallic, or "fantasy", finishes. The traditional craft of gilding takes care and time to master, although the results are well worth the effort involved. Happily, new materials – such as substitute metals, metallic powders in various colours, and modern spray paints – now make it easier for the non-expert to explore this rewarding area. The following section lists the most important materials you need for gilded or other metallic finishes:

Bronze, aluminium and silver powders These fine particles of metal can be mixed with varnish or blown or brushed on to water-based size.
Dutch metal leaf This looks like gold leaf but is much cheaper and is made from a copper and zinc alloy.
Gilding water This liquid is made from water, methylated spirit and rabbit skin size and is used in water gilding.
Gold leaf Gold leaf is available as loose or transfer leaf. Both types come in books of 25 leaves. Gold leaf is available in many tones, weights and thicknesses and is classed in carats.
Gold and silver paints These are made in the same way as liquid leaf but from cheaper materials. They are useful for stencilling and decorative painting.
Liquid leaf The mixture of metallic powder and deep red primer can be used to cover a wide variety of surfaces.
Methylated spirit This spirit is used to dilute gilding water and for

ABOVE *The gilder's materials, including undercoats, gold leaf and metallic powders.*

distressing or ageing gilded surfaces.
Shellac and polishes These come in many guises, such as button polish and transparent polish. Shellac is the ideal way of enhancing the hue of Dutch metal and other substitute leaf.
Silver, copper and aluminium leaf These leaves are 15 cm/6 in square and come in books of 25–500 loose or transfer sheets.
Varnishes Oil-based and water-based varnishes come in various finishes , ranging from matt to satin and gloss.
Water-based size This fast-drying synthetic size goes tacky after 15–20 minutes. It can be used with bronze powders and substitute leaf.
White spirit This oil-based solvent is used to dilute oil-based paints and varnishes and to clean up afterwards.

GILDING

There is a wide range of materials that give the appearance of traditional gilding at a fraction of the price. Liquid leaf, gold powders, pastes and sprays are available from most good art suppliers and framing shops, and come in a wide selection of metallic hues. Liquid leaf is fast drying and easy to use, while gold sprays should be a staple of any supply cabinet. French enamel varnish can be used on all these materials.

Liquid leaf

1 Apply an oil- or water-based primer to the surface to be gilded and let dry. Paint on a base coat in the desired colour and leave to dry.

2 Shake the bottle of liquid leaf well and brush on to the surface with a real bristle brush. Leave to dry (about 20 minutes). Seal with varnish.

Pastes

1 Apply an oil- or water-based primer to the surface to be gilded and leave to dry. Paint on a base coat in the desired colour and dry. The base colour will enhance the final tone of the gold.

2 Apply the paste to the surface using a cloth or brush. Rub it in well, paying particular attention to any areas of detail. Leave to dry.

3 Rub the surface with a soft cloth, then seal with a wax or polish and polishing rubber if required.

Paints and sprays

1 Apply an oil- or water-based primer to the surface and leave to dry. Paint or spray on a base coat in the desired colour and leave to dry. The base colour will enhance the final tone of the paint or spray.

2 Shake the paint can or spray can well. If painting, paint an even coat on to the surface and leave to dry. Repeat if necessary. If spraying, work in a well-ventilated area and hold the can 30 cm/ 12 in from the surface. Leave to dry.

3 Spray or paint does not need to be varnished, but an amber shellac or coloured French enamel varnish will enhance the colour.

PINPRICKED LAMPSHADE

This is a satisfying way to turn a plain paper lampshade into something special. Switching on the light transforms the delicate pricked design into a magical pattern of stars.

YOU WILL NEED

MATERIALS
tracing paper
paper
lampshade
masking tape

EQUIPMENT
pencil
scissors
towel
darning needle
cork (optional)

1 Trace the templates from the back of the book, enlarging if necessary. Copy them several times and cut out roughly from paper.

2 Arrange the motifs in a repeating pattern on the outside of the lampshade and secure with masking tape. Trace the shape of the stuck-on motifs on the inside of the shade.

3 Rest the shade on a towel and, working from the inside, gently pierce the design with a needle. You can bind the needle with masking tape or stick it into a cork to make it easier to hold. Finish the design with a scalloped edging.

CHILD'S CHAIR

Ladybirds are always welcome in their paintbox-bright uniforms. Add fun and interest to an ordinary white chair by getting a procession of the little creatures to meander across it. This simple decoration will make it any child's favourite seat.

YOU WILL NEED

MATERIALS	EQUIPMENT
thin card or paper	*pencil*
child's chair	*scissors*
acrylic paints: red and black	*fine and decorator's*
oak and clear acrylic varnish	*paintbrushes*
	cloth

1 Draw and cut out a simple template in the shape of a ladybird's head and body from card or paper. Draw around it with a pencil, making the ladybirds trail up and across the child's chair.

2 Using a fine paintbrush, fill in the bodies of the ladybirds with red paint. Allow to dry completely.

3 Draw around the ladybirds and add the heads, legs and spots using black paint and a fine paintbrush. Allow to dry completely.

4 Thin the oak varnish with water and paint it on using a decorator's paintbrush. Rub off immediately with a clean cloth. Apply a coat of clear varnish to finish.

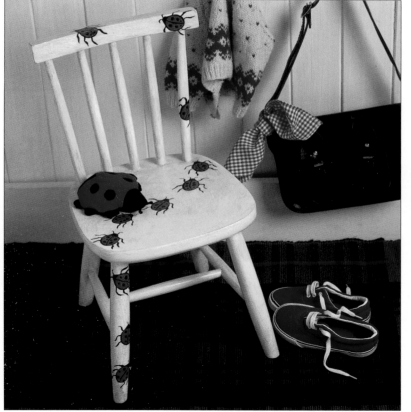

GILDED LAMP

A silver gilded lamp base and a golden shade form a light source that will be a glowing focal point in any room. When lit, the gilded lamp seems to shimmer; the effect in a dark corner is magical.

YOU WILL NEED

MATERIALS
turned-wood lamp base
red oxide primer
3-hour oil size
aluminium leaf
white card
parchment coolie shade,
45 cm / 18 in
PVA (white) glue
Dutch gold leaf transfer book
black watercolour paint
methylated spirits-based
varnish

EQUIPMENT
paintbrushes
large stencil brush
craft knife
cutting mat
pencil
cotton wool

1 Prime the lamp base with red oxide and allow to dry. Paint the lamp base with size and allow to dry for three hours. When the size is "squeaky", it is ready for gilding. Lay the aluminium leaf on the base and rub with a stencil brush so it adheres to the base. Repeat until the lamp base is covered.

2 Draw the sunflower motif freehand on to white card. Carefully cut out a stencil from the card with the craft knife. Trace the outline on to the base, through the stencil, with a sharp pencil.

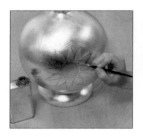

3 Paint the size on to the stencilled sunflower shapes and leave it to dry for three hours, until "squeaky".

4 Meanwhile, paint a small area of the lampshade with slightly diluted PVA (white) glue. Straight away, lay a sheet of Dutch gold on top and rub with the stencil brush, so it adheres. Quickly brush off any excess.

5 Repeat with another small area, applying Dutch gold as before.

6 Continue until the shade is covered. Seal the shade with another coat of diluted PVA (white) glue.

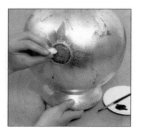

7 When the size on the base is "squeaky", cover the design with a sheet of Dutch gold and rub gently with the stencil brush, so that the gold adheres to the size. Brush off any excess.

8 Put a little watercolour paint on a piece of cotton wool and rub it into the centre of the sunflower, to give a mottled or stippled effect. Finally, give the whole base a coat of varnish.

COFFEE CANISTER

Rescue an old kitchen canister and give it a new identity as a piece of folk art. Painted tinware was very popular with the early American settlers, and pedlars would roam the countryside loaded with brightly coloured cans, jugs and bowls that they sold from door to door.

YOU WILL NEED

MATERIALS
kitchen canister
emulsion (latex) paints: brick-red, black and bright red
clear gloss varnish

EQUIPMENT
sandpaper
fine paintbrushes
plates
foam roller
tulip stamp

1 Rub back the kitchen canister with sandpaper. Paint the canister and lid with brick-red emulsion (latex) paint. Allow to dry, then paint the rim of the lid black.

2 Spread some black paint on to a plate and run the roller through until it is evenly coated. Ink the tulip stamp and print a tulip on the side of the canister, carefully tilting the stamp block around the curve of the canister.

3 Fill in the tulip using bright red paint.

4 Apply several coats of gloss varnish to seal and protect the canister. Leave each coat to dry thoroughly before applying the next.

ORIENTAL BOWL

Blue and white ceramics are a centuries-old tradition with the classic Oriental willow garden pattern and its many variations being the most famous. Use this bowl to display a bunch of fresh flowers or some pot-pourri.

YOU WILL NEED

MATERIALS
*white glazed bowl
ceramic paints: light, medium and dark blue
polyurethane varnish*

EQUIPMENT
*magic marker
ruler
paintbrushes
paint-mixing container
craft knife
damp cloth*

1 Mark a horizontal line 6 cm/2½ in down from the rim of the bowl. Draw decorative scrolls above the line. To create an overall pattern, draw parts of motifs cut off by the rim and base.

2 Paint the scrolls in light blue. Try to keep the tone evenly flat and dense. Allow to dry, then paint medium blue over all the remaining area above the horizontal line. Allow to dry.

3 Scratch around the edges of the light blue with a craft knife to reveal the white below. Paint a dark blue line around each scroll. Leave as much of the white as visible as possible. Allow to dry.

4 Using dark blue, paint the base up to its rim. Leave the rim white. Aim for a flat, solid tone. Allow to dry, then varnish the bowl to finish.

CANDLE POT

*There is nothing like candlelight and, for a room
with a natural or maritime theme, this candle
pot is the perfect finishing touch.*

YOU WILL NEED

MATERIALS	EQUIPMENT
florist's tape	*craft knife*
thick candle	*glue gun and glue sticks*
mossing pins or stub wires	
oasis	
flowerpot	
dried moss	
seashells	
starfish	
dried flowerheads	

1 Stick tape around the base of the candle. Hold three evenly spaced mossing pins or bent stub wires against the tape and tape over them, to hold in position.

2 Trim the oasis to fit tightly in the flowerpot. Push it in and secure it firmly with some of the leftover pieces. Push the pins into the oasis to hold the candle firmly.

3 Glue the dried moss around the candle. Then add the shells all around. Place them evenly and keep standing back to check the balance.

4 Add the more delicate materials, such as the starfish and dried flowerheads, to the top to finish off.

STENCILLED ROLLER BLIND

Stylized, almost abstract, oranges and lemons on this stencilled blind give it a fifties feel. It would look great in a kitchen decorated with strong, fresh vibrant colours.

YOU WILL NEED

MATERIALS
tracing paper
stencil card
plain white cotton fabric,
to fit window
masking tape
acrylic gouache paints:
orange, yellow, lime-green,
black and red
roller blind fabric stiffener
roller blind kit

EQUIPMENT
pencil
craft knife
cutting mat
scissors
stencil brush
large paintbrush
paper towels

1 Trace the template from the back of the book, enlarging it so that the repeat design will fit across the width of your blind, and trace it. Transfer it three times to stencil card. Using a craft knife, cut out only the areas you will need for each stencil: 1) the lemons, oranges and red spots; 2) the leaves; 3) the black details.

2 Lay out the white fabric on a smooth flat surface and secure with masking tape. Using gouache paints, stencil the oranges and lemons motif all over the fabric. Keep the stencil brush as dry as possible, blotting off any excess paint on paper towels and cleaning the stencil if paint starts to bleed under the edges.

3 Leave the orange and lemon motifs to dry, then proceed with the remaining colours. Paint the leaves next, then the red spots (using the first stencil) and finally the black details.

4 When dry, paint the fabric with fabric stiffener following the manufacturer's instructions. Hang the fabric on a washing line to dry, keeping it very straight. Make up the blind using the blind kit.

PAINTED CHAIR

It is usually easy to find an old chair at a reasonable price, and with a stencil pattern like the one used here, it can soon be transformed into a charming piece of furniture fit for any room in the house.

YOU WILL NEED

MATERIALS
chair
matt emulsion (latex) paints:
pumpkin-yellow, white and
brick-pink (optional)
tracing paper
stencil card
spray adhesive
various artist's acrylic or
stencil paints
paper
clear water-based varnish
small tubes of raw umber and
raw sienna artist's acrylic paint

EQUIPMENT
paintbrush
paint-mixing container
cloth
pencil
stencil brush
pale-coloured chalky pencil
long-haired artist's brush
fine-grade steel wool

1 If your chair is bare wood, apply an even coat of light pumpkin-yellow (add a touch of white to lighten it); if you are covering old paint, first apply a coat of brick-pink paint as a base for the chair.

2 Thin the pumpkin-yellow with water and apply to the chair. Use a damp cloth to wipe some of it off. It will remain in the grain to emphasize the mouldings. Trace the template from the back of the book and transfer to stencil card.

3 Spray the back of the stencil lightly with adhesive and position it centrally on the chair back. Apply the colours sparingly, rubbing the paint through the stencil with circular strokes.

4 Use a chalky pencil to draw radiating guidelines in the centre of the lower chair back. Practise the strokes on paper, using a long-haired brush. Starting with the tip of the brush in the centre, draw it towards you, gently pressing down in the middle of the stroke to make a teardrop shape.

5 Line the chair with thick and thin stripes. Add water until the paint flows easily off your brush.

6 When drawing lines, try to complete the whole line with a single brushstroke. Begin with the shortest and least conspicuous lines, progressing to the more obvious ones as your skill grows. Add rings of colour to highlight any turned features in the chair.

7 Rub back the paint with steel wool to simulate wear and tear. Don't overdo it and just concentrate your efforts on the edges. Tint the clear varnish with a small amount of raw umber and raw sienna and apply two coats, leaving to dry between coats. Apply one final layer of tinted varnish.

SUNFLOWER MOSAIC

Shards of china and mirror wink in the sun on this attractive and unusual wall decoration. Collect bright fragments of china in a harmonious blend of colours for your design.

YOU WILL NEED

MATERIALS
plywood sheet, 5 mm/¼ in
electric cable
masking tape
PVA (white) glue
white undercoat paint
china fragments
mirror strips
tile adhesive
grout
cement dye

EQUIPMENT
pencil
coping saw or fretsaw
medium- and fine-grade
sandpaper
bradawl
wire-cutters
paintbrush
tile nippers
rubber gloves and dust mask
grout-mixing container
nailbrush
soft cloth

1 Draw out the sunflower on the plywood. Cut it out with a saw and sand any rough edges. Make two holes with a bradawl. Strip the cable and cut a short length of wire. Push the ends of the wire through the holes from the back and fix the ends with masking tape at the front. Seal the front with diluted PVA (white) glue and the back with white undercoat.

2 Cut the china and mirror strips into irregular shapes, using the tile nippers. Stick them to the plywood, using tile adhesive. Dip each fragment in the adhesive and scoop up enough to cover the sticking surface; the adhesive should squelch out around the edge of the mosaic, to make sure it adheres securely. Allow to dry thoroughly overnight.

3 Wearing rubber gloves and a dust mask, mix up the grout with cement dye, following the manufacturer's instructions. Press a small amount of wet grout into the gaps. Allow to dry for about five minutes. Brush off any excess with a nailbrush. Leave again for five minutes and then polish with a clean, soft cloth. Allow to dry overnight.

STIPPLED STORAGE TINS

Cheer up a plain set of metal containers to give your kitchen shelves a bright new look. The tins are painted with a stipple technique which gives a textured, sponged effect.

1 Wash the tins and lids, and spray them with several coats of white matt paint. Mark wavy lines at the top and bottom of each tin. Fill in either side of the lines with yellow and green paint. Use a dry brush and a stippling action, adding some areas of darker colour. Experiment by mixing the colours together to achieve the shades you prefer.

2 Trace the template from the back of the book, enlarging if necessary, and transfer it to the central panel of the tin. Add extra sections of the design so that it fits all the way around. Paint the large trefoil leaves green and the small leaves rust-brown.

3 Paint a dark brown band on either side of the leaf panel. Add a few blue dots in the spaces. Outline the leaves with darker shades of brown and green, then paint the tendrils brown. Paint the main part of the lid green, picking out the details in brown and blue. Finish off by spraying the tin with a protective matt varnish. Allow to dry thoroughly.

PAINTED FLOWERPOTS

Terracotta flowerpots have a chunky robust quality which makes them ideal for holding candles. Use them in their natural state to make lovely impromptu container candles for alfresco evenings, with friends and family.

YOU WILL NEED

MATERIALS
flowerpots
acrylic paints: yellow, gold and blue

EQUIPMENT
flat and fine paintbrushes

1 Using a broad, flat paintbrush, paint the flowerpot yellow both outside and inside.

2 Paint the inside of the pot with one layer of gold.

3 Using a very fine brush, decorate the outside of the pot with blue paint.

SUNFLOWER HOOK BOARD

This board is both useful and attractive. Mount it on the wall near the back door so spare keys are always to hand and easily found.

YOU WILL NEED

MATERIALS

pine plank, 1 cm/½ in
white undercoat paint
acrylic paints: blue, grey, white, red, yellow and green
3 brass hooks

EQUIPMENT

pencil
ruler
pair of compasses
coping saw or fretsaw
medium- and fine-grade sandpaper
paintbrushes
paint-mixing container
drill, with number 10 bit

1 Mark out the shape of the board on the wood. It is 9.5 cm/3¾ in wide, 10 cm/4 in high to the shoulder and 13 cm/5 in high to the top of the curve. Use a pair of compasses to draw in the curved top.

2 Cut out the board and sand any rough edges. Paint with undercoat. When dry, sand lightly. Paint the board with the base colour, using a mixture of blue, grey and white to give a rustic mottled effect.

3 When the base is dry, sketch in a flower shape freehand, in pencil. Paint the flower white. Colour in the flower, mixing colours as necessary. Paint the stem green. When the paint is dry, sand it lightly with fine sandpaper to give a "distressed" finish. Drill a hole in the top centre of the board and screw in the brass hooks along the bottom.

D R I E D   F L O W E R   W R E A T H

In the spring the new, straight growth of woodland trees and shrubs is ideal for collecting and making into a wreath. Cut the twiggy stems early in the year before the buds have opened.

YOU WILL NEED

MATERIALS

*36 thin twigs, about 60 cm/24 in long
mid-blue acrylic paint
fine florist's wire
2 cm/¾ in wide blue and white check ribbon, 3 m/3 yd
6 pink dried or silk roses
selection of dried flowers and plant material in pink, purple and blue
all-purpose glue
small, variegated ivy leaves*

EQUIPMENT

*scissors
paintbrush*

1 Trim the ends off the twigs to make them all about 45 cm/18 in long. Paint each stick blue and allow to dry.

2 Overlap two bundles of six sticks and tie the ends securely with wire. Add a third bundle to complete the triangle. Weave the remaining bundles through the first triangle to make a six-pointed star and tie the ends with wire.

3 Wind the ribbon around the central hexagon and tie off neatly at the back. Build up the design, using the roses and small sprigs of pink, purple and blue plant material. Use glue to secure. Stick several ivy leaves at each corner of the hexagon.

4 Wrap a short piece of ribbon around five points of the star. On the sixth point, tie a longer piece into a loop.

CANDLESTICK

Candlesticks are available in many different shapes and sizes and they can be given a rich, aged effect with the use of the various shades of Dutch metal leaf. Try looking for candlesticks in junk shops where you may come across more unusual pieces.

YOU WILL NEED

MATERIALS	EQUIPMENT
wooden candlestick	*paintbrushes*
red oxide spray primer	*burnishing brush or soft cloth*
water-based size	*steel wool*
gold Dutch metal leaf	*paint-mixing container*
methylated spirit	*soft cloth*
amber shellac varnish	
acrylic paints: red and	
yellow-ochre	

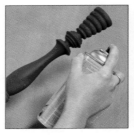

1 Spray the candlestick with an even coat of red oxide primer, making sure that all the details and recesses are fully covered. Allow to dry for about 30–60 minutes.

2 Paint on a thin, even layer of water-based size and leave for 20–30 minutes, until it becomes clear and tacky.

3 Carefully lay the gold leaf on to the surface to cover the whole area. Burnish it with a burnishing brush or cloth to remove the excess leaf and bring up a lustre.

4 Dip some steel wool into a little methylated spirit and gently rub the raised areas and details of the candlestick to distress the surface, taking care not to rub too hard.

5 Seal with a thin, even layer of amber shellac varnish and allow to dry for about 45–60 minutes.

6 Mix the red and yellow-ochre paint with some water. Paint it on to the surface and allow to dry for 5 minutes. Rub off most of the paint with a cloth, allowing only a little paint to remain in the areas of detail. Dampen the cloth if the paint has set too much. Allow to dry.

PAPIER-MACHE WALL PLAQUE

This engaging crab relief is easily made from moulded papier-mâché and it looks very effective as a hanging decoration.

YOU WILL NEED

MATERIALS
strong card
wire, for hanging
masking tape
newspaper
wallpaper paste
paper pulp
white emulsion (latex) paint
self-hardening clay
acrylic or poster paints:
turquoise-blue, navy blue,
pink and yellow
gloss varnish

EQUIPMENT
scissors
ruler
wire-cutters
clay-modelling tool
paintbrushes

1 Cut out a piece of card about 13 cm/5 in square. Cut a short piece of wire and bend it into a hook shape. Attach to one side of the card with masking tape.

2 Soak 2.5 cm/1 in squares of newspaper in wallpaper paste and apply to both sides of the card. When dry, apply paper pulp to the border area. Allow to dry.

3 Apply a coat of white emulsion (latex) paint. When dry, use self-hardening clay to make relief decorations and a frame, shaping it with a modelling tool. Leave to harden.

4 Paint the crab and the border in acrylic or poster paints, then seal with several coats of varnish.

WASTEPAPER BIN

Complete a baronial look in your sitting-room or study with a suitably ennobled bin.

YOU WILL NEED

MATERIALS

tracing paper
paper
foam or corrugated card,
6 mm/¼ in thick
wastepaper bin
cotton piping cord
acrylic gesso
thin card
acrylic paints: red, yellow
and dark green
shoe polish: brown, black
and neutral
paper towels
gold size
Dutch gold leaf transfer book
polyurethane varnish

EQUIPMENT

pencil
scissors
craft knife
cutting mat
glue gun and glue sticks
fine and thick paintbrushes

1 Trace the templates from the back of the book, enlarging them if necessary, and cut out of paper. Draw the shield motif four times on the foam and cut out with a craft knife. Stick the shields on to the sides of the bin with the glue gun. Cut lengths of cotton cord to go around the shields and tie at the bottom in a bow. Stick them on with a glue gun.

2 Paint the whole piece, inside and out, with two coats of acrylic gesso. Paint a piece of thin card with gesso and, when dry, draw around the cross template four times on this. Mix red, yellow and green acrylic paint to resemble red oxide primer and paint the shields and the top edge of the bin.

3 Using a large brush in a weeping movement, apply patches of brown and black shoe polish, each mixed with neutral to tone them down, over the white gesso, including the string and the cross motifs. Wipe the polish off with paper towels as you go, to build up the antiqued effect. Cut out the crosses. Paint a thin layer of gold size on the red oxide areas.

4 When it is nearly dry, gently apply the gold leaf and rub it down through the backing paper with your thumbnail. Rub harder in some areas to reveal the red oxide beneath. Put a spot of gold leaf in the centre of each cross motif. Glue a cross to the centre of each shield. Coat inside and out with polyurethane varnish.

SPONGE-PRINTED SHELF

Shelf-edgings are a lovely decorative detail for a country-style kitchen or breakfast room. Even if you do not possess the perfect heirloom dresser, you can make the plainest of shelves beautiful in this way.

YOU WILL NEED

MATERIALS
tracing paper
thin card
sponge
13 cm/5 in strip unbleached
calico, length of shelf
spray fabric stiffener
fabric paints: red, yellow and
green
6 cm/2½ in strip green print
cotton fabric, length of shelf
matching sewing thread
double-sided tape

EQUIPMENT
pencil
scissors
felt-tipped pen
ruler
paintbrush
iron
dressmaker's pins
sewing machine
needle

1 Trace the templates from the back of the book, enlarging them so that the triangular shape measures about 13 cm/5 in across. Transfer the fruit and leaf outlines to thin card and cut them out. Draw around them on to the sponge and cut out the shapes.

2 Mark a row of triangles along one edge of the calico, spray with fabric stiffener and allow to dry. Cut along the pencil lines. Use the sponge blocks to print the design. Print a leaf on each side of the fruit.

3 Stipple darker areas on the fruit and leaves.

4 With wrong sides facing, press the green fabric in half lengthways, then press under 5 mm/¼ in along one long edge. With right sides facing, sew the other raw edge to the top of the shelf edging with a 5 mm/¼ in allowance. Fold the green fabric over to cover the top and slip stitch the folded edge to the back of the seam. Neaten the corners and then tape to the shelf.

YELLOW ROSES LAMPSHADE

A hand-decorated lampshade makes the perfect finishing touch to any room scheme. This particularly charming one has roses made from textured paper that are enhanced when the light is switched on.

YOU WILL NEED

MATERIALS
*tracing paper
yellow and green textured
paper
fabric lampshade
PVA (white) glue
matt water-based acrylic
varnish*

EQUIPMENT
*soft and sharp pencils
fine black felt-tipped pen
scissors
paintbrush*

1 Trace the templates from the back of the book, enlarging if necessary. Go over the lines again with a black pen.

2 Lay the yellow paper over the motif and trace the outline showing through, using a pencil. Cut carefully along the lines and lay the pieces out on a flat surface. Trace and cut out the green pieces in the same way.

3 Stick the shapes on to the shade, spreading a thin layer of glue on the reverse of each piece as you go. Using the traced rose as a guide, stagger the motifs over the lampshade.

4 Glue the calyx and stem under each rose. Once dried, paint the shade with two coats of varnish.

IVY STOOL

This very delicately painted little seat would look charming in the leafy surrounds of a garden room.

YOU WILL NEED

MATERIALS
wooden stool
white emulsion (latex) paint
tracing paper
acetate sheet
masking tape
acrylic paints: sap-green and white
clear gloss acrylic varnish

EQUIPMENT
sandpaper
paintbrushes
pencil
permanent magic marker
craft knife
cutting mat
stencil brush
paint-mixing container

1 Sand the stool and paint it with two or three coats of white emulsion (latex) paint. Trace the templates from the back of the book. Tape the acetate over the design and draw the outlines of the leaves with a magic marker.

2 Cut out the stencil carefully using a craft knife.

3 Using sap-green acrylic paint mixed with a little white, stencil the leaves all over the stool. Allow to dry.

4 Using sap-green acrylic paint and a fine brush, paint the tendrils, outlines and veining on the leaves. Finally, protect the stool with two or three coats of gloss varnish.

IVORY CUPID

Plaster blanks are now readily available, and can be customized with the paint finish of your choice. Here, the plaster has been given an antique ivory finish, but you could experiment with distressed metallic effects, such as gold or verdigris.

YOU WILL NEED

MATERIALS	EQUIPMENT
shellac sanding sealer	paintbrushes
plaster cupid	paint-mixing container
raw umber emulsion	paper towels or soft cloth
(latex) paint	

1 Paint shellac sanding sealer all over the cupid. Leave the sealer to dry for 30 minutes, then apply another coat, and allow to dry again.

2 Dilute the raw umber paint with water, until it is the consistency of double (heavy) cream. Paint the cupid all over with watered-down emulsion (latex) paint.

3 While the paint is still wet, rub it off using paper towels or a soft cloth, so that the paint only remains in the crevices. Be sure to use a clean spot each time you rub, or you will put the paint back on.

PAINTED BENCH

Every home should have a bench like this, to squeeze extra guests around the dinner table and to keep by the back door for comfortable boot-changing. This bench is made from reclaimed floorboards which give it just the right rustic feel.

YOU WILL NEED

MATERIALS
bench
shellac
emulsion (latex) paints:
dark blue-grey, deep red
and light blue-green
antique pine colour varnish
clear matt varnish

EQUIPMENT
medium-grade sandpaper
paintbrushes
small piece of sponge

1 Sand the bare wood on top and underneath and seal it with a coat of shellac. Allow to dry thoroughly and apply a second coat.

2 Paint the legs in dark blue-grey emulsion (latex) paint, working directly on to the wood. Allow to dry.

3 Paint the seat with deep red emulsion (latex) paint.

4 Use the sponge to dab an even pattern of blue-green spots across the whole surface of the seat.

5 When the paint is thoroughly dry, rub the seat and edges with sandpaper to simulate wear and tear.

6 Apply a coat of antique pine varnish to the whole bench. Then apply two coats of matt varnish for a strong, solid finish.

SUNFLOWER PLATTER

These hand-painted flowerheads give a truly exuberant decorative finish to a plain terracotta flowerpot base. You could also use the same idea to decorate a matching pot for a floral container display. Ceramic pots and bases come in many different sizes and they are ideal for painting on. Use ceramic paints for a translucent quality, or acrylics for a brighter, bolder look.

YOU WILL NEED

MATERIALS
ceramic flowerpot base
white undercoat paint
acrylic paints: red, yellow,
brown and green
matt varnish

EQUIPMENT
paintbrushes
pencil
paint-mixing container

1 Apply undercoat to the flowerpot base. Sketch out your pattern freehand in pencil. Fill in the whole background in red acrylic paint and fill in the flowers in yellow.

2 Use a fine paintbrush to draw the outlines for the detail in the central flower.

3 With a fine brush, fill in the detail in the central and other flowers, in brown and green. When dry, give the whole platter two or three coats of varnish, leaving to dry well between coats.

GILDED LAMPSHADE

The delicate laciness of filigree work inspired the elegant design for this lampshade. The success depends on arranging cut-out motifs pleasingly, so keep an eye out for decorative paper with suitable designs. You need two papers, one of a lighter weight than the other, such as tissue paper and wrapping paper.

YOU WILL NEED

MATERIALS	EQUIPMENT
cupid-patterned wrapping paper	*paintbrushes*
gold-patterned tissue paper	*paint-mixing container*
PVA (white) glue	*clean cloth (optional)*
lampshade	
gold acrylic paint	

1 Carefully tear around the cupid shapes in the wrapping paper. Tear smaller areas from the gold-patterned tissue paper, for contrast.

2 Mix equal parts PVA (white) glue and water. Coat the lampshade with this to seal it. Paint the PVA (white) glue on to the reverse of the cupid shapes and stick them around the shade. The glue may stretch the paper, so smooth out any wrinkles with a clean cloth (or leave them for added texture).

3 Fill in the areas that are left with gold-patterned paper, overlapping to make sure the shade is completely covered. Finally, seal the paper all over with more diluted PVA (white) glue.

4 When dry, decorate the edge of the lampshade with gold paint.

PLASTER DECORATIONS

Decorating a plain wall with plaster shapes is unusual in itself, but adding gilding to the shapes makes them even more individual.

YOU WILL NEED

MATERIALS
*PVA (white) glue
plaster shapes
waterproof ceramic adhesive
masking tape
white acrylic wood primer
white emulsion (latex) paint
acrylic paints: yellow-ochre
and rose
acrylic scumble glaze
water-based size
gold Dutch metal leaf
water-based varnishing wax*

EQUIPMENT
*decorator's paintbrushes
ruler or plumb-line
paint-mixing container
burnishing brush or soft cloth*

1 Mix two parts PVA (white) glue with one part water and seal the plaster shapes with this mixture, working the sealant into the recesses. Allow to dry for two hours.

2 Use a thick, even coat of ceramic adhesive to stick the shapes to the panel or wall. Allow to dry. Hold the shapes in place with masking tape while the glue is drying, if necessary.

3 Paint the panel or wall with white acrylic primer and allow to dry for several hours. Paint on a coat of emulsion (latex) paint and allow to dry.

4 Measure off the positions of the stripes on the panel or wall. Use a ruler or plumbline to mask off the first stripe with masking tape. Reduce the tackiness on a piece of cloth first.

5 Mix one part yellow-ochre paint with six parts scumble glaze. Apply to the area between the masking tape, using random brushstrokes and allowing plenty of the base colour to show through. Allow to dry.

6 Remove the masking tape and re-mask along the outside edge of the glazed stripe. Mix one part rose paint with six parts scumble glaze. Paint the second strip in the same way as the first, and allow to dry.

7 Paint a thin, layer of water-based size on to the plaster shapes and leave for 20–30 minutes, until it becomes clear and tacky.

8 Place a sheet of gold leaf on to the sized surface and press lightly into the detail, ensuring that the whole shape is covered.

9 Burnish the shapes with a burnishing brush or soft cloth to remove the excess leaf.

10 Seal with a thin, even coat of varnishing wax and allow to dry.

JEWELLERY

Making your own jewellery is a very satisfying craft, giving you the chance to make the end result exactly what you want. The variations and possibilities for highly original jewellery pieces are endless, and the suggestions in the following section – more than 20 in all – can be adapted to suit your personal taste.

Jewellery can be crafted out of a variety of materials, from polymer clay to papier-mâché and from fibreboard to fine gold, silver or copper wire. Most of the equipment and material required is readily available from craft suppliers – or you can hunt around at home for old beads and interesting gems to transform into glittering jewellery.

BASIC TECHNIQUES

Wire, in various metals and gauges, is a favourite material among craft jewellery makers. Copper and silver-plated wire can be easily coiled to make attractive bracelets, earrings and necklaces, while jewellery wire is used for connecting parts of jewellery pieces. Coils are the most commonly decorative device in wire jewellery making. They also have a practical use as they neaten and make safe what would otherwise be sharp.

ABOVE *A selection of different-sized wires, including silver-plated copper wire and aluminium wire.*

Closed coils

1 Using small round-nosed pliers, make a small loop at the end of the wire.

2 Hold the loop firmly with parallel pliers. Use them to bend the wire around until you have a coil of the size required. Keep adjusting the position of the pliers as you work.

Open coils

1 Using round-nosed pliers, make a small loop at the end of the wire. Holding the loop in the pliers, place your thumb against the wire and draw the wire across it to form a curve.

2 Use your eye to judge the space left between the rings of the coil.

3 Finally, carefully flatten the coil with parallel pliers.

MATERIALS AND EQUIPMENT

Aluminium wire is a dull blue-grey colour. It is easy to work with as it is soft and bends easily.

Beads and gemstones must be flat backed and, if they are to be baked, made of glass.

Buttons are useful for decorating jewellery. Be on the lookout for odd luxury buttons on old jackets.

Copper wire has a lovely warm colour and it comes in many degrees of hardness.

Cords and braids can be used on jewellery. Use fine gold cord for hanging jewellery as a decoration.

Enamelled copper wire is ideal for jewellery making as it comes in a wide range of colours.

Epoxy resin glue is used in two parts and is a strong glue.

Jewellery wire is used for connecting pieces for earrings and necklaces.

Paints can be applied to polymer clay to provide your jewellery with the colour of your choice.

Polymer clay comes in a variety of colours and finishes and can be used in a number of ways.

Silver-plated copper wire comes in coils in many different gauges and is particularly suited to jewellery making.

Threads are useful for jewellery making. Make sure you have a good supply of different shades and thicknesses to add variety to your work.

Varnish can be used to provide the finishing touch to a piece of painted clay jewellery.

MINIATURE BROOCH

Polymer clay is a marvellous medium for moulding:
it is much easier to use than clay and can be baked
hard in an ordinary oven. The colours are jewel-like
in their intensity and yet this hand-made brooch has
a charming naïvety, reminiscent of folk art.

YOU WILL NEED

MATERIALS	EQUIPMENT
polymer clay: carmine, green	*rose nail*
and golden-yellow	*kitchen foil*
earring posts	*small rolling pin*
epoxy resin glue	*kitchen knife*
brooch pin	*trefoil-shaped aspic cutter*

1 Roll three small balls of carmine clay for each rose. Flatten a ball and wrap it around the rose nail. Overlap the petals as you work and gently open out the bud

with your finger. Ease off the nail and insert an earring post. Push into a ball of foil. Make another four roses in the same way. Bake in a preheated oven at 110°C/225°F/Gas ¼ for about 10–15 minutes.

2 Roll out the green clay thinly. Cut small squares and fringe one edge. Wrap this around the base of the rose to form the calyx. Cut out several trefoil shapes. Cut three leaves from each and mark veins with the knife.

3 Roll out a 2 x 5 cm/¾ x 2 in rectangle of yellow clay for the vase. Lay thin pieces of carmine and green clay on top as decoration. Roll the pieces flat and mark with a knife.

4 Press leaves around the roses and put in the vase. Put leaves on the edge. Bake in the oven at 110°C/225°F/Gas ¼ for 30 minutes. When cool, glue on the pin.

ORANGE SLICE EARRINGS

Bright, jolly earrings to suit the mood of a hot summer's day, or cheer up a dull one. Have fun making the orange slices as realistic as you can — these ones even have pips.

YOU WILL NEED

MATERIALS	EQUIPMENT
polymer clay: pearl, pale orange and dark orange	*craft knife & cutting mat*
	bamboo skewer
earring findings: eye pins,	*rolling pin*
earring hooks and large rings	*old cheese grater*
	round-nosed jewellery pliers

To assemble each earring: loop the wire from the small orange and snip off any excess. Put a large ring through the orange slice and attach to the small orange. Attach the earring hook above the small orange.

1 Roll a 5 mm/¼ in diameter sausage of pearl clay. Roll the pale orange clay into a sausage of 1.5 cm/⅝ in diameter and cut it lengthways into four triangular segments.

2 Cut lengthways into two of the triangles and insert a skewer. Press the clay together to form a tunnel. Fill the tunnel with the sausage of pearl clay and reform the triangular shape.

3 Roll some dark orange clay thinly and cut 1 cm/½ in strips for between the segments. Arrange to make a semicircle. Roll out a 3 mm/⅛ in layer of pearl and a 2mm/1/12 in layer of dark orange for the peel and mould around the edge.

4 Make two 1 cm/½ in balls in dark orange and roll on a grater to make them look like oranges. Fit an eye pin through the centre of each. Trim any overlapping edges from the large segment and roll the peel on a grater. Cut two 5 mm/¼ in slices and make a hole in each for the earring hook. Bake all the pieces at 110°C/225°F/Gas ¼ for 20–30 minutes.

GLITTERING BROOCH

This delightful brooch is cleverly made from the humblest of materials: corrugated card and newspaper.

YOU WILL NEED

MATERIALS
paper
corrugated card
newspaper
wallpaper paste
PVA (white) glue
white acrylic primer
gouache paints: light blue,
yellow and red
gloss varnish
gold enamel paint
brooch pin
epoxy resin glue

EQUIPMENT
pencil
craft knife
cutting mat
bowl
paintbrushes

1 Draw a star shape on to paper and transfer the design to the corrugated card. Cut out the star shape. Soak some newspaper in wallpaper paste, scrunch it up and mound it onto the star.

2 Cover the whole brooch in layers of newspaper pieces soaked in wallpaper paste and allow to dry.

3 Give the brooch a coat of PVA (white) glue, then one of white acrylic primer. Allow to dry, then paint on the design and protect the brooch with a coat of clear gloss varnish.

4 Add gold enamel paint details. Finally, fix a brooch pin to the back using epoxy resin glue.

FRUITY BRACELET

Paint a summery bracelet with pretty oranges and lemons. This example is decorated with many slices of different citrus fruits.

YOU WILL NEED

MATERIALS
tracing paper
thin card
large hook and eye
masking tape
paper pulp
strong clear glue
gold foil (from a chocolate wrapper)
acrylic paints: white, yellow, red and orange
gold paint
clear gloss varnish

EQUIPMENT
pencil
scissors
paintbrushes
paint-mixing container

1 Trace the template from the back of the book, enlarging it to fit your wrist, and cut out of thin card. Tape a large hook and eye to either end.

2 Cover the card with layers of paper pulp, making sure the masking tape and all the edges are neatly covered. Allow to dry. Use strong, clear glue to stick a sheet of gold foil to the inside of the bracelet. Trim the edges.

3 Prime the outside of the bracelet with a coat of white acrylic paint to smooth the surface. Decorate with slices of citrus fruit using acrylic paints. Add touches of gold paint around the edges, pips and dimples.

4 When the paint is dry, protect it with a coat of clear gloss varnish.

HEART BROOCH AND PIN

This little brooch is made from fibreboard and is gilded using a distressed technique. The delicate pin will make the perfect finish to a wedding hat. It is made from modelling clay, gilded and decorated with pretty jewels.

YOU WILL NEED

MATERIALS
fibreboard,
10 x 10 cm/4 x 4 in
pale blue spray paint
water-based size
gold Dutch metal leaf
methylated spirit
acrylic varnishing wax
brooch back
modelling clay
hat pin and cap
gilt cream
plastic jewels

EQUIPMENT
black magic marker
coping saw
sandpaper or chisel
2 bristle brushes
burnishing brush or soft cloth
steel wool
soft cloth
glue gun and glue sticks
rolling pin
clay-modelling tools

1 Draw a heart shape freehand on to the fibreboard using a black magic marker. Cut out and roughen the edges with sandpaper or a chisel to add some texture.

2 Spray both sides of the heart with pale blue spray paint and dry. Paint on a thin, even layer of water-based size and leave for about 20–30 minutes, until it becomes clear and tacky.

3 Lay the gold leaf on to cover the heart. Burnish it with a burnishing brush to remove the excess leaf and bring up a lustre. Distress the surface using steel wool and methylated spirit.

4 Seal with acrylic varnishing wax and allow to dry. Buff with a soft cloth. Glue a brooch on to the back of the heart.

5 Warm and roll out the clay to 5 mm/¼ in thick. Cut out a heart shape and round off the edges. Use modelling tools to make indentations and patterns in the clay.

6 Insert the hat pin into the heart. Enlarge the hole by circling the pin, then remove it. Bake the heart in the oven, following the manufacturer's instructions.

7 Rub gilt cream into both sides of the heart and allow to dry, before buffing with a soft cloth.

8 Glue the hat pin into the base of the heart and glue plastic jewels on to the heart.

WINGED CUPID BROOCH

This exotic piece of jewellery is made from paper pulp, hand-painted in gorgeous colours, then decorated.

YOU WILL NEED

MATERIALS
tracing paper
thin card
paper pulp
wallpaper paste
newspaper
PVA (white) glue
white acrylic primer
flat-backed glass gems
epoxy resin glue
eye-hook pins
selection of gouache paints
clear matt varnish
gold enamel paint
small glass tear-drop beads
small jump-rings
brooch fixing

EQUIPMENT
pencil
craft knife & cutting mat
paintbrushes
dressmaker's pin
paint-mixing container
round-nosed jewellery pliers

1 Trace the template from the back of the book, and transfer to card. Cut it out and cover with paper pulp. Apply five layers of wallpaper paste and newspaper strips. Allow to dry.

2 Coat with PVA (white) glue and then white primer. Allow to dry between each stage. Glue the glass gems on with epoxy resin. Make holes with a pin and insert the eye-hook pins, securing them with epoxy resin.

3 Paint on your design with gouache paints. When dry, coat with matt varnish. Allow to dry again, then add the gold enamel details.

4 Assemble all the brooch pieces and tear-drop beads, joining them with jump-rings, using the pliers. Glue the brooch fixing into position.

GOLD WIRE EARRINGS

These delicate earrings take the form of tiny sets of scales. The miniature baskets are filled with beads in shades of green and blue. Be sure to thread the same number of beads into each basket so that the scales balance when you are wearing the earrings.

YOU WILL NEED

MATERIALS
fine brass beading wire
selection of small glass beads:
blue and green
4 jump rings
2 split rings
pair of posts with loops
short length of
0.8 mm brass wire
pair of butterfly backs

EQUIPMENT
fine crochet hook
round-ended jewellery pliers
round-ended pencil
wire-cutters

1 Using the fine beading wire, crochet four round shapes 1 cm/½ in across. On the last round make three 2 cm/¾ in equally spaced loops. Leave a long end of wire. Twist the loops with jewellery pliers.

2 Mould each round into a dome shape with a pencil. Thread equal numbers of beads on to the loose end of wire and secure them in each basket. Do not trim the wire yet.

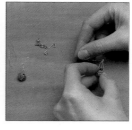

3 Attach a jump ring, then a split ring to each earring fitting. Cut two 4.5 cm/1¾ in lengths of the thicker wire. Twist an upward loop in the centre of each, then bend each end down into two loops from which the baskets will hang.

4 Attach the centre loop to the split ring using another jump ring. Thread the long end of wire on one basket through the top of the twisted loops to bring them together and attach to the bar. Repeat with the other baskets. Finally, trim the ends of wire.

WOODEN BEAD NECKLACE

Simple wooden balls available from craft shops are transformed by gilding to make this glittering necklace. Experiment with leaf or powders in different colours, and alternate the beads on the string for stunningly original jewellery. This necklace could also make an unusual tie-back.

YOU WILL NEED

MATERIALS
assorted wooden balls
small nails
wood off-cut
red oxide spray primer
water-based size
Dutch metal leaf: gold, copper
and aluminium
amber shellac varnish
acrylic varnishing wax
leather thongs

EQUIPMENT
vice
drill, with fine bit
hammer
paintbrushes
burnishing brush or soft cloth
scissors

1 Holding each ball in turn in a vice, drill a hole through the centre.

2 Hammer small nails into the off-cut of wood to make a rack. Place the balls on the nails and spray them with red oxide primer. Allow to dry completely.

3 Paint a thin, even layer of water-based size on to the balls and leave to rest for about 20–30 minutes, until the size becomes clear and quite tacky.

4 Gild the balls in different colours of metal leaf and burnish with a burnishing brush or soft cloth to remove the excess leaf.

5 Seal the gold balls with amber shellac varnish and the copper and aluminium balls with acrylic varnishing wax. Buff the wax with a soft cloth after several hours to bring up the lustre.

6 Cut lengths of leather thong and thread the balls on to it, alternating each colour. Tie the ends of the thong in a knot.

S P I D E R ' S   W E B   B R O O C H

Reproduce the delicate texture of a web in glittering copper and silver wire. The resident spider is resplendent in blue and gold and not at all threatening, especially as she has only got six legs and a curly tail!

YOU WILL NEED

MATERIALS

1 mm/0.039 in copper wire
0.65 mm/0.024 in silver wire
modelling clay
2 small glass beads
strong glue
brooch pin
turquoise acrylic paint
clear varnish
gold powder

EQUIPMENT

wire-cutters
round-nosed jewellery pliers
clay-modelling tool
paintbrush

1 Cut four 8 cm/3 in lengths of copper wire. Curl both ends of each piece into a loop with the pliers.

2 Arrange the pieces to form a star. Wrap the silver wire around the centre. Working outwards in a spiral, twist the silver wire once around each copper wire. Secure and trim.

3 Cut six 6 cm/2½ in lengths of copper wire. Curl one end of each into a loop, then bend into the shape of the spider's legs.

4 Cut an 8 cm/3 in length of wire and bend into a spiral for the tail. Roll two balls of clay for the body and head.

5 Press the two clay balls together, joining securely with the help of the modelling tool. Smooth the surface of the clay with wet fingers or the modelling tool.

6 Insert the looped ends of the wire legs and tail into the spider's body. Press two glass beads into the head to make the eyes.

7 Press the spider's body on to the wire web. Flatten a small piece of clay and attach it to the spider from underneath the web, using the modelling tool to join it securely. Leave the clay to harden.

8 Glue the brooch pin to the back of the spider and secure the legs and tail with drops of glue. Paint the body and head turquoise and allow to dry. Apply a coat of varnish to seal the paint. Mix gold powder with a little varnish and apply swiftly with a dry brush to leave some of the turquoise paint showing through.

SUNFLOWER BADGE

This cheerful sunflower face can be worn as a badge or brooch and would enhance a plain sweater or jacket. The bright colours would go equally well with black or neutral-coloured clothes.

YOU WILL NEED

MATERIALS
*birch-faced plywood sheet,
5 mm / ¼ in thick
wood glue
white undercoat paint
acrylic paints: yellow, red,
chocolate-brown and gold
gloss varnish
brooch pin*

EQUIPMENT
*pencil
pair of compasses
coping saw or fretsaw
medium- and fine-grade
sandpaper
paintbrushes
paint-mixing container*

1 Using a pair of compasses draw a circle for the flower-centre on the plywood. Draw the petals freehand around the centre. Draw another circle the same size as the centre. Cut out these two shapes with a saw.

2 Sand any rough edges on the flower. Sand the circle's edge to a curve. Glue the circle to the centre of the flower shape, with wood glue. Paint with white undercoat and allow to dry. Sand lightly.

3 Paint in the flower details with the acrylic paints. Mix yellow and red to make a golden-yellow for the petals. Paint the centre brown. When dry, add gold dots to the centre. Apply a coat of gloss varnish. When the varnish is dry, stick the brooch pin on to the back of the badge with wood glue.

SUN AND MOON BADGES

Wear one of these jolly badges as a colourful and bold brooch on a plain coat or sweater. Simple to make, these badges are bound to lift everybody's spirits in the early morning.

YOU WILL NEED

MATERIALS
tracing paper
birch-faced plywood sheet,
5 mm /¼ in thick
white undercoat paint
acrylic paints: yellow, red and blue
gloss varnish
epoxy resin or hot glue
2 brooch pins

EQUIPMENT
pencil
coping saw or fretsaw
medium- and fine-grade sandpaper
paintbrushes
paint-mixing container

1 Trace the templates from the back of the book, enlarging if necessary, and transfer the outlines to the plywood. Cut out the shapes with the saw and sand the edges smooth.

2 Paint both sides and all the edges of the shapes with white undercoat. When the paint is dry, sand it lightly.

3 Paint the fronts of the sun and moon with acrylic paint and add the features and other details. When dry, add a coat of varnish and allow to dry. Put a thick line of glue on the back of each badge and press the brooch pin firmly into the glue.

SPARKLING BROOCH

Layers of contrasting fabrics and glittering machine embroidery make this a spectacular item of jewellery. The rough texture of the felts is wonderfully highlighted by the shimmering organza and metallic machine embroidery.

YOU WILL NEED

MATERIALS
*thin card or paper
purple felt
rust felt
shot organza
metallic embroidery threads
sewing thread
brooch findings: back plate and
pin*

EQUIPMENT
*scissors
dressmaker's pins
tailor's chalk
sewing machine, with
embroidery foot
needle*

1 Draw two freehand starfish shapes, one larger than the other, on to thin card or paper. Cut the templates out roughly. Pin the large starfish template to the purple felt and draw around it with tailor's chalk.

2 Cut out irregular pointed shapes from the purple and the rust felt. Pin them down into the points of the starfish outline. Cut out the small starfish shape from the shot organza and pin it on top of the felt starfish.

3 Thread the machine with metallic thread and stitch over the edges of the organza. Build up layers of texture and colour with different threads.

4 Cut out the starfish brooch shape and stitch a small felt circle on to the centre-back. Stitch on the brooch findings.

SHOOTING STAR BADGE

This jolly little shooting star will brighten up any outfit. Use pearlized paint for its tail and glossy varnish to make the colours glow.

YOU WILL NEED

MATERIALS
tracing paper
birch-faced plywood sheet, 5 mm / ¼ in thick
white undercoat paint
acrylic paints
water-based paints
pearlized paints
gloss varnish
all-purpose glue
brooch pin

EQUIPMENT
pencil
fretsaw
sandpaper

1 Trace the template from the back of the book and transfer to the plywood. Cut out and sand all the edges.

2 Paint with a coat of white undercoat. When dry, sand lightly and mark the remaining points of the star in pencil.

3 Paint on the badge's design in acrylic paints, using pearlized paint for the tail. Protect it with gloss varnish.

4 Glue the brooch pin to the back of the badge.

EMBROIDERED JEWELLERY

*Glittering embroidery,
iridescent paper, and
shimmering beads
combine to make this
very special jewellery.*

YOU WILL NEED

MATERIALS

*water-soluble fabric
tracing paper
iridescent paper
metallic sewing threads
paper towels
modelling clay
blue-green watercolour inks
metallic paints
spray varnish
selection of small beads
2 jewellery split rings
2 earring wires or posts
2 jewellery jump rings*

EQUIPMENT

*embroidery hoop
dressmaker's pins
pencil
vanishing fabric marker
sewing machine
scissors
iron
stiff wire
paintbrush
card
felt
plastic sheet
beading needle
flat-nosed jewellery pliers*

Craft tip
You need a sewing machine
that can be used without a
foot for free embroidery
(most can). Sewing through
the iridescent paper does
blunt needles, so have some
spares ready. You can buy
water-soluble fabric from
good craft shops.

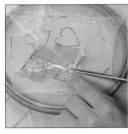

1 Stretch a layer of the fabric
in the hoop and pin another
layer to the back. Trace the
template from the back of
the book, enlarging if
necessary. Trace them on to
the fabric with the vanishing
marker. For the centres, pin
iridescent paper to the back
of the fabric.

2 Thread the machine with
metallic thread and
experiment with sewing
without a foot, using
different thread thicknesses,
to achieve the right tension.
Machine around the heart
centres and cut away any
excess paper from the back.

7 Cover a piece of card with
felt and plastic, to make a soft
backing sheet. Pin the motifs
to the sheet and spray the
clay beads and motifs with
the varnish.

3 Machine around the
outline, first in straight stitch
and then in zigzag stitch. Go
over the design several times,
so it is quite stiff.

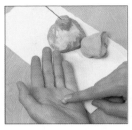

5 Make small balls of clay for
the beads, and push them on
to a stiff wire. Allow to dry,
stuck into a piece of clay.

8 Attach metallic thread to
the top of the earring.
Thread on two small beads,
then a clay bead, and two
small beads. Take the thread
through a split ring and then
down again through the
beads and into the motif.
Fasten off. Sew beads on to
the centres of the motifs.

4 Dissolve the fabric in some
water according to the
manufacturer's instructions.
Iron dry between paper
towels.

6 Paint the beads with
water-colour inks. When
dry, add dots of metallic
paint, to highlight them.

9 To join the earring fixings,
open up a jump ring with
pliers and thread through the
split ring. Join it to the ring
on the earring. For a
pendant, thread a machine-
embroidered chain through
the slip ring.

SUN AND MOON EARRINGS

These very striking earrings shimmer with a distressed black and gold paint effect that is simple to achieve but looks stunning. The faces are easily modelled out of clay and you only need to leave them to dry thoroughly before you paint them, for a durable finish. The earrings would enhance any formal outfit, or add a touch of glamour to casual clothes.

YOU WILL NEED

MATERIALS
*modelling clay
strong clear glue
2 earring findings: backs and
butterflies
black acrylic paint
gold powder
matt varnish*

EQUIPMENT
*rolling pin
jar lid
clay-modelling tools
fine-grade sandpaper
fine paintbrushes
paint-mixing container*

1 Roll out two pieces of clay to about 5 mm/¼ in thick and 8 cm/3 in in diameter. Use the jar lid as a template to mark an inner circle. With a modelling tool, gradually build up the central area so it is higher than the outer area but still flat.

2 Model the features of your sun with a modelling tool. Mark the rays around the face and cut away any excess clay. Pierce dots in the face and rays. Allow to dry for several days. Model a moon in the same way.

3 Glue the earring backs in position. Sand between the rays for a smoother look. Paint black. Mix the gold powder with the varnish, then paint. With a semi-dry brush, go over the face up and down quickly, so that the black underneath shows through and accentuates the face.

SATIN HAT DECORATION

Decorate a straw hat for a summer wedding or garden party with a vibrant rose made of satin ribbon. Combine ribbons of different widths and colours to make a bunch of roses or stick to one beautiful specimen that will catch every eye.

YOU WILL NEED

MATERIALS
satin ribbons in
3 complementary shades
matching sewing threads
28-gauge green florist's stem
wires
green ribbon
green crepe paper or
florist's tape

EQUIPMENT
scissors
needle

1 Make each petal separately, starting with the centre one. Cut a piece of ribbon, twice the width of the ribbon in length, and fold it with wrong sides together. Fold over each of the top corners twice and stitch them down invisibly. Repeat to make enough petals for a rose, using different shades and widths of ribbon.

2 Roll the centre petal around itself and secure it with a stitch. Insert a stem wire into this petal and continue to add petals around the rose, stitching together as you go.

3 Finish the rose by binding with green ribbon, to hide the raw edges. Stitch it in place at the top, just over the base of the petals, and then gather up the lower edge neatly and stitch to secure. Bind the stem with crepe paper or florist's tape.

ABSTRACT HAIRSLIDE

Silver leaf is applied to glow-in-the-dark polymer clay which is then embossed with the spiral patterns of some old earrings to create an intriguing effect. In the dark, a subtle glow emanates from the tiny cracks in the silver leaf.

YOU WILL NEED

MATERIALS
glow-in-the-dark polymer clay
thin card
silver leaf
old jewellery or buttons
dark blue bronze powder
slide clip
varnish
strong glue

EQUIPMENT
rolling pin
pencil
scissors
craft knife
cutting mat
brayer
dust mask
paintbrushes

1 Roll out some clay to a thickness of 5 mm/¼ in. Draw the shape you want freehand on thin card and cut it out. Place the card on the clay and cut out the shape with a craft knife.

2 Apply silver leaf to the clay shape by passing a brayer over it.

3 Create a regular pattern around the edge of the silver-leafed clay by pressing interestingly shaped old jewellery or buttons into it to leave indentations.

4 Fill in the central area of the brooch with a random pattern applied in the same way as in step 3, but using different shapes, if liked.

5 Wearing a dust mask, lightly brush the surface all around the edge with some bronze powder.

6 Slip a small piece of thin card through the full width of the slide clip, then place the decorated clay shape on top. The clay will mould itself to the curved shape of the slide but the card will prevent it sagging too much.

7 Bake it in this position, following the manufacturer's instructions. When it is cool, varnish the surface and glue it back on to the slide clip.

EMBROIDERED HATPIN

A decorated hatpin is an easy way to jazz up a plain hat. This one features an elaborately embroidered velvet sun backed with beaten brass.

YOU WILL NEED

MATERIALS
yellow velvet
fine strong fabric
contrasting cotton threads
contrasting metallic machine-
embroidery threads
brass sheet
brass wire
epoxy resin glue
beads
hatpin

EQUIPMENT
scissors
embroidery hoop
sewing machine, with
darning foot
tin snips
metal file
small, round-nosed hammer
small anvil
wire-cutters
round-nosed jewellery pliers

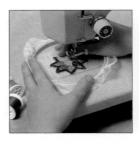

1 Cut out a yellow velvet sun. Place a piece of fine fabric in an embroidery hoop and machine stitch the sun to it. Thread the machine with contrasting threads in the top and bobbin and whip stitch around the edge. Then make a deeper band of stitching around the edge. Stitch spirals in contrasting metallic threads, then stitch the face.

2 Cut a sun from the brass sheet with tin snips and file the edges smooth. Hammer to give texture. Bend a spiral at each end of a piece of wire and hammer flat. Position the wire spirals in the centre front of the sun shape and glue a circle of brass just in the centre, over the ends of the wire.

3 Trim the velvet sun away from the fine fabric and glue it in the centre of the brass sun. Thread some beads on the hatpin and glue them in place. To assemble, bend the spirals slightly backwards and slide the hatpin through the top and bottom spirals.

DIAMOND EARRINGS

These earrings are made from appliquéd silk and organza pieces, embroidered in a combination of colours and textures to give a jewel-like quality.

YOU WILL NEED

MATERIALS	EQUIPMENT
thin card	*scissors*
small pieces of calico, organza and silk	*fabric marker or pen*
	dressmaker's pins
coloured and metallic machine embroidery threads	*sewing machine, with darning foot*
wadding (batting)	*needle, size 80/12*
PVA (white) glue	*embroidery hoop*
metallic acrylic paint	*paintbrush*
2 eye pins	*needle*
2 metallic beads	*jewellery pliers*
2 glass beads	
2 ear wires	

1 Draw two diamond shapes on card and cut out. Cut out two of the diamond shapes from calico. Draw four horizontal lines inside each diamond. Cut two slightly larger organza diamonds and pin them over the marked shapes.

2 Place the fabric in a hoop. With matching thread, stitch the horizontal lines and several lines around the design. Trim away the excess organza close to the stitched outline.

3 Cut two small pieces of silk in a contrasting colour and pin over the diamond shapes. Place the piece in a hoop and stitch several lines around the horizontal stripes with matching thread. Trim away any excess fabric close to the stitch line.

4 Work several stitch lines around the appliquéd stripes to cover the raw edges. Work more stitch lines around the design with metallic thread.

5 Pin a second piece of calico to the wrong side of the embroidery. Place it in the hoop, and stitch around three sides of each diamond. Stuff both shapes with wadding (batting), poking it into the corners. Stitch the fourth side to close the gap. Cut out the shapes close to the stitched outline.

6 Work several stitch lines around the appliquéd stripes to cover the raw edges. Work more stitch lines around the design with metallic thread.

7 With a small brush, apply glue to the edges of the shapes to varnish and stiffen the piece. Allow to dry, then paint in a metallic acrylic paint. Allow to dry.

8 Make a hole at the top of each diamond with a needle. Thread each eye pin through a small metallic bead, a glass bead and then the diamond. Twist the wire at the back and attach the ear wires and eye pins.

JEWELLERY POUCH

The intense dark red of the velvet here provides a suitable setting for your most precious jewels but it also evokes the softness and tonal contrasts of rose petals, which are stylized into a free-embroidered motif to decorate the pouch.

YOU WILL NEED

MATERIALS
wadding (batting)
dark red velvet
taffeta lining fabric
tracing paper
matching sewing thread
paper
velvet ribbon
small button

EQUIPMENT
tape measure
dressmaker's scissors
dressmaker's pins
sewing machine, with darning foot
pencil
fabric marker
needle

1 Cut pieces of wadding (batting) and lining fabric, 38 x 25 cm/15 x 10 in. Assemble the pieces and pin together with the velvet in the middle. Stitch seams

across the top and bottom. Turn the pouch right sides out so the wadding (batting) is inside, and pin the top and bottom seams.

2 Trace the template from the back of the book, enlarging if necessary. Transfer the rose and leaf motifs to the fabric. Select the darning or free embroidery mode on the machine. Stitch the design.

3 With right sides together, stitch the two short edges together to form a tube, leaving the lining unstitched. Fold under the lining and slip stitch the edges together.

Cut a paper circle with a 7.5 cm/3 in radius. Use it to cut pieces of velvet and taffeta.

4 With right sides together, stitch around the seam allowance, leaving a 4 cm/ 1½ in gap. Clip the seam allowance and turn the circle the right way out. Stitch the circle to the bottom edge of the tube. Cut a 40 cm/16 in length of ribbon. Stitch the centre point to the side seam of the bags, and sew a small button in place.

R I B B O N   H A I R B A N D

Choose ribbons to match a bridesmaid's outfit or a special party dress. With practice, these pretty ribbon roses are easy to make.

YOU WILL NEED

MATERIALS
6 cm/2½ in wide tartan ribbon, 60 cm/24 in matching sewing thread
4 cm/1½ in wide sheer green plain and gold-edged ribbons, 2 m/2 yd
satin-covered padded hairband
4 cm/1½ in wide gauze and satin ribbons, 38 cm/15 in

EQUIPMENT
needle
scissors

1 Make the central rose first. Fold one end of tartan ribbon at a right angle and twist it around twice, to form the centre. Secure at the bottom with a few stitches. Form the first petal by twisting the ribbon around the centre, folding it back at a right angle, so that the top edge lies across the "stalk", and stitch to secure.

2 Continue to wrap the ribbon round in this way, securing each petal with a stitch. Finish off firmly, by stitching through all the ribbon layers.

3 Cut the green ribbon into 15 cm/6 in lengths and fold to make leaves. Sew them to the centre of the hairband and attach the rose.

4 Make six more roses in different colours and sew them along the hairband, interspersing them with more leaves in both plain and gold-edged ribbon.

PAINTED TIN BADGES

A good way to use up small scraps of tin is to make brooches. These can be very simple in construction and made special with painted decorations. The enamel paints are very opaque and they cover previous coats of paint beautifully, so light colours can be painted on top of dark very successfully.

YOU WILL NEED

MATERIALS
scrap of 30 gauge/0.01 in tin
enamel paints
clear gloss polyurethane
varnish
epoxy resin glue
brooch fastener

EQUIPMENT
magic marker
work shirt and protective
leather gloves
tin snips
bench vice
file
wet and dry sandpaper
china marker
fine paintbrushes

1 To make the brooch front, draw a circle freehand measuring 5 cm/2 in diameter on a piece of tin. Wearing a work shirt and gloves, cut out the circle with tin snips.

2 Clamp the circle in a bench vice and file the edges. Finish off the edges with damp wet and dry paper so that they are completely smooth.

3 Draw the outline of the sun on to one side of the brooch with a china marker. Paint around the outline with enamel paint, then fill in the design. Allow to dry.

4 Paint in the background, then paint the sun's features on top of the first coat of paint, using a fine paintbrush and enamel paint. Set aside and allow to dry.

5 Seal the surface of the brooch with two coats of clear varnish to protect it from scratches. Allow to dry thoroughly between coats.

6 Mix some epoxy resin glue and use it to stick a brooch fastener on to the back. Let the glue dry thoroughly before wearing the brooch.

SILVER STAR EARRINGS

A clay mould is used to model these eye-catching silver earrings, so it's easy to make as many as you want – as gifts for everyone who admires them on you!

YOU WILL NEED

MATERIALS
modelling clay
tracing paper
thin card or paper
pair of earring studs
all-purpose glue
black acrylic paint
silver powder
clear varnish

EQUIPMENT
rolling pin
pencil
clay-modelling tools
paintbrushes

1 Roll out a small piece of clay to a thickness of 8 mm/⅜ in.

2 Trace the template from the back of the book, enlarging if necessary, and transfer it to thin card or paper. Cut the star out of the clay.

3 Mark a line from the centre of the star to each point where two rays meet and use the flat side of the modelling tool to mould each point to a 90-degree angle. Smooth the star with water, tuck the edges in neatly and allow to dry.

4 Take a small ball of clay and press with your palm until it is about 2 cm/¾ in thick. Press in the hardened clay star, then lift it out carefully without distorting the mould. Allow to dry thoroughly.

5 Use the mould to make further clay stars. Lift them out of the mould and place face up on the work surface.

6 Trim off any excess clay with a modelling tool. Allow to harden.

7 Glue earring studs to the backs of the stars.

8 Paint the stars with black acrylic paint and allow to dry thoroughly.

9 Mix silver powder with varnish and brush over the stars to complete.

CLOCKS AND MOBILES

Making clocks might not be the first idea that springs to mind when you want to create an object for your home, but it's easier than it sounds. The materials are all readily available, and this section provides step-by-step instructions on how to put them together to make a timepiece of your choice.

Mobiles have always been loved by children, and the ideas in this book will also appeal to adults. When making mobiles, it is important to get the suspension measurements accurate as otherwise they may not balance as effectively as they should.

BASIC CLOCKMAKING

This section shows that beautiful clocks can be created simply, without special skills, using that modern invention, the quartz movement. Simply attach a clock face and hands to the quartz movement and you have a timepiece that will keep accurate time for a year and a half on one small battery. The body of the clock can be made from almost any material and in any shape that you desire. The joy of these projects is that you can choose the style of clock to fit in with your particular craft skills.

ABOVE *Different styles of hands and numerals allow flexibility in matching the clock face to the design of the clock.*

The body of the clock

The clock is made up of the following components: the movement, spindle, hands, dial and numerals. Numerals can be left off if preferred or replaced with symbols, letters or pictures.

The movement

Quartz movements are measured in millimetres (or inches in the US). They come in a variety of sizes, so that the bigger the movement, the longer and heavier the hands may be. They appear to work whichever way up they are put, and they are not too sensitive to damp and heat, so they may be fixed in a kitchen or bathroom.

BELOW *Assembling a clockface.*

The spindle

The spindle, or shaft, sticks out of the middle of the movement and passes from the front to the face of the clock. The hands are fitted on the spindle. The length of the spindle is important if the clock is to fit together, so remember to work out the thickness of the clock before fixing the length of the spindle.

The hands

Hands come in many shapes and sizes; they can be made of plastic or metal, or can be ornate or plain.

The dial

You do not necessarily have to have a conventional, numbered dial on a clock, although it's best to mark the four main points of 12, 9, 6 and 3.

The numerals

Numerals normally come in Roman or Arabic typefaces, but they can also be formed from dots or any other motif you like. Buy them as individual self-adhesive numbers, as discs or on a dial.

Choosing the movement

As a rough guide, short spindles fit up to a 3 mm/⅛ in thickness, medium up to 10 mm/⅜ in, and anything thicker needs a long spindle. For accuracy, it is advisable to take a sample of your face materials with you when you buy the spindle.

Fitting the hands and movement

Most quartz clocks and fittings are similar to each other and are very easy to fit. Drill a 10 mm/⅜ in hole in the clock and put the movement on the back; screw the fixing nut (most clocks come with a fixing nut) into the movement from the front. Then carefully push the hands on to the end of the spindle, taking care you don't bend the hands. Put in the battery and test to ensure that the hands will move freely.

MOBILE HINTS AND TIPS

Mobiles can be made from almost any light material that can be suspended. Florist's foam is light and easy to carve. Cotton waste balls can be painted and decorated with beads and sequins to make glittering baubles. Papier-mâché shapes are easily made from old newspaper. Perhaps the easiest mobiles are those made from shapes cut directly from card. Sewn fabric and felt toy shapes make brightly coloured mobiles for babies and children.

More unusual materials for mobile pieces include baked salt dough and modelling clay (in small amounts); dried fruits, flowers, herbs and spices also make pretty elements for instant kitchen mobiles.

Mobile frames

The most traditional frame for a mobile is made up of a series of bars suspended from a long central bar. Materials to use include dowelling, knitting needles, skewers, kebab sticks, bamboo canes, pencils and chopsticks.

Crossbars are a popular way of hanging mobiles with five hanging shapes. Hang a shape from the end of each arm and the fifth from the centre. Crossbars can be made from wood, card or wire. Wooden crossbars are made more solid if a rebate (rabbet) or groove is cut in the centre of each bar before gluing together. Add a tack or bind with thread to form a strong joint.

A circular frame can be made from wire, card or the stiffener used for boning theatrical costumes. The circle can then be painted or covered in fabric. For a small mobile, a large curtain ring might be suitable.

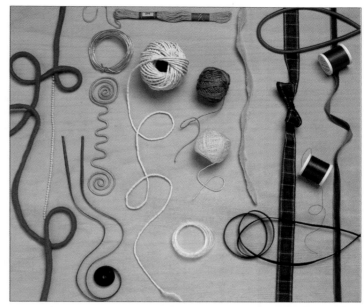

ABOVE *Be creative with the choice of supports for your mobile – wires for strength and structure, pretty ribbons and threads for colour and contrast.*

Threads and wires

The thread or wire chosen to hang the shapes is an important element of the overall design. An "invisible" thread such as nylon fishing line will give the effect of the mobile elements floating in the air. Coloured embroidery silk, thread or wool can contrast with brightly coloured shapes.

Wire is the best choice for a more structured, controlled mobile. Useful wires include galvanized wire, florist's wire, jewellery wire and coat hangers. The ends of the hanging wires can be bent into hooks to fit into holes made in the frame and the hanging elements.

Hanging threads can be decorated with beads and sequins. Tie knots in the thread to space the beads. Each mobile project in this section clearly describes the materials you will need to achieve the most effective result.

ABOVE *If you intend to hang your shapes from a length of fairly rigid wire, you can always attach a separate, more malleable wire loop or hook to hang your frame on to.*

ABOVE *A double knot fastens the shape so that it is ready to be attached to the frame. Fishing line is a good choice as it is both strong and virtually invisible.*

HERALDIC SYMBOLS MOBILE

There are plenty of strong, simple shapes in heraldry, just right for cutting out to hang on this fascinating mobile. The small motifs on a heraldic shield are called "charges". Pick out the raised detailing on each shape in gold to catch the light subtly.

YOU WILL NEED

MATERIALS
tracing paper
stiff card
newspaper
wallpaper paste
acrylic gesso
acrylic paints: cobalt-blue,
yellow, orange, red, purple and
black
28 earring pins
super glue
gold magic marker
fine thread
1 cm/½ in wooden dowel,
36 cm/14 in long
2 large wooden beads
2 brass screws
gold paint
3 red tassels
length of red cord

EQUIPMENT
pencil
craft knife
cutting mat
metal ruler
scissors
glue gun and glue sticks
paintbrushes
fine- and coarse-grade
sandpaper
drill
screwdriver
needle

1 Trace the template from the back of the book to measure 30 cm/12 in across, and transfer the design to card. Cut out the main shapes.

2 Cut out the charges with scissors. Tear strips of newspaper and coat them with wallpaper paste. Cover the banner with a layer of papier-mâché.

3 Allow to dry, then apply a second layer of newspaper strips. Once this is dry, create the raised designs on the motifs using a glue gun.

4 Paint the pieces with two coats of gesso, sanding lightly between layers. Mark diagonal stripes on the banner and paint alternate stripes in cobalt-blue.

5 Insert an earring pin in the centre top of each charge and secure with a few drops of super glue. Attach an earring pin at each corresponding point on the banner in the same way.

6 Paint the charges in heraldic colours. Highlight the raised design with a gold pen. Once the pieces are dry, assemble the mobile using fine thread. Apply a drop of glue to each knot.

7 Drill a hole in each end of the dowel. Flatten one end of each bead by rubbing with coarse sandpaper, then screw the beads to each end of the dowel. Coat with gesso and paint gold.

8 Stick three earring pins on the top of the banner. Tie to the dowel. Sew a tassel to each cored end and slip the loops over the beads. Glue to the dowel. Pin a third tassel to the bottom of the banner.

COPPER MOBILE

The glowing warmth of copper catches the light very gracefully as the mobile moves. The mobile looks spectacular and yet is easily worked in wire and thin sheet metal. To help you form the cupid figure, try drawing it out on paper first and then use your drawing as a guide for bending the wires.

YOU WILL NEED

MATERIALS	EQUIPMENT
paper	pencil
thin copper sheet,	scissors
15 x 4 cm/6 x 1½ in	tin snips
thin copper wire, 3 m/3 yd	wet and dry sandpaper
medium copper wire, 1 m/1 yd	hammer and nail
fine gold-coloured wire,	round-nosed pliers
1 m/1 yd	
epoxy resin glue	

1 Draw a heart and arrow freehand on paper and cut them out. Trace three hearts and one arrow head and flight on to the copper sheet.

2 Cut the shapes out with tin snips and sand the edges smooth to the touch with wet and dry sandpaper.

3 Pierce holes in the hearts by hammering a nail through the metal.

4 Use the pliers to bend a cupid shape from the thin copper wire. In this design the cupid is made in two sections: the head, torso and arm are made from one length of wire, and the legs from another. Bend the medium copper wire into a bow shape.

5 Attach the two parts of the cupid with short lengths of thin wire.

6 Bend three heart shapes from the thin copper wire. Attach the copper hearts to the inside of the wire hearts with lengths of gold-coloured wire.

7 Bend the arrow head to make a groove in which the shaft will lie. Do the same with the flight. Cut a 15 cm/6 in length of medium wire for the shaft and glue it in place.

8 Use gold-coloured wire to create the string of the bow and connect it to the bow. Insert the arrow between the cupid's fingers and connect the bow to its chest. Cut two pieces of medium wire, 12 cm/ 4¾ in and one 25 cm/ 10 in for the struts. Bend the ends into loops. Assemble the mobile using the gold wire.

OCTOPUSSY

This is an inexpensive and easy way to make a mobile – brightly coloured paper is simply torn and stuck together to form the bold sea creatures. This mobile is bound to delight children and will certainly brighten up a bedroom or bathroom.

YOU WILL NEED

MATERIALS
tracing paper
thin card
papers, brightly coloured on one side
PVA (white) glue
thread

EQUIPMENT
pencil
scissors
hole punch

1 Trace the octopus template from the back of the book, enlarging if necessary. Transfer to card and cut out two of them. Draw freehand and cut out eight fish, squid and starfish shapes.

2 Fold the paper with the coloured side innermost. Draw around each of the card shapes and tear out slightly outside the pencil line. You should now have two copies of each shape.

3 Glue the paper to both sides of each card shape. Tear out eyes, fins, tails and scales. Glue on. Cut a slot in each octopus body. Punch a hole at the end of each arm and two holes in the head. Punch a hole at the top edge of each sea creature.

4 Slot together the octopus pieces. Attach the shapes with thread and suspend from the top of the octopus's head.

SPIDER WEB CLOCK

Find gold-coloured hands for your clock, which will match the gilded spider and contrast prettily with the rich blue background.

YOU WILL NEED

MATERIALS
5 mm/¼ in birch plywood, about 18 x 18 cm/7 x 7 in white undercoat paint acrylic paints: dark blue, white, black and gold clear matt varnish clock movement and hands

EQUIPMENT
pair of compasses pencil ruler drill fretsaw or coping saw sandpaper paintbrushes paint-mixing container white marker pencil

1 Draw a circle on the plywood and divide it into eight segments using a ruler. Draw the looping outline of the web around the edge.

2 Drill a hole in the centre and saw around the edge of the web. Sand, then paint with white undercoat. Allow to dry and sand again.

3 Paint the clockface in dark blue and stipple with a stiff brush while the paint is still wet. Apply a coat of varnish. When dry, draw the web pattern with a white marker pencil.

4 Mix a light grey colour and paint over the web using a fine brush. Paint on the flies and the golden spider. Finish with a coat of matt varnish and attach the clock movement and hands.

PALMISTRY MOBILE

Stars, spirals and rings spring from this mystical hand. The vibrant decoration is enhanced with light-reflecting mirror glass.

YOU WILL NEED

MATERIALS
tracing paper
thin card
newspaper
masking tape
galvanized wire
wallpaper paste
mirror glass
chemical metal filler
PVA (white) glue
white acrylic primer
liquid gold leaf paint
gloss polyurethane varnish
small brass screw hooks
epoxy resin glue
gouache paints
small brass jump rings
picture wire

EQUIPMENT
pencil
craft knife
cutting mat
wire-cutters
round-nosed pliers
hammer
paintbrushes

1 Trace the templates from the back of the book, enlarging if necessary, and cut out all the shapes from card. Crumple small pieces of newspaper and tape them to each shape to create the form. Leave the wings of the hand and the small stars flat. Using round-nosed pliers, coil and bend a piece of wire, following the template, and tape to the sun shape.

2 Using wallpaper paste, cover each shape in several layers of newspaper. Allow to dry.

3 Break the mirror by placing it between several layers of newspaper and hitting it gently with a hammer. Mix the chemical filler according to the manufacturer's instructions. Apply to one side of each wing and along the top of the hand, then carefully press in the pieces of mirror. Allow to dry, then repeat on the other side of the wings. If you like, stick one small piece of mirror on to each of the small star shapes.

4 Cut five lengths of wire and coil into "S" shapes, following the template. Coat with PVA (white) glue, white acrylic primer and gold paint, then varnish. Allow to dry after each coat. Screw one small hook into each of the papier-mâché shapes, into the tip of each finger and into each wing of the hand. Screw four hooks into the sun piece. Secure the hooks with epoxy resin glue. Coat the shapes with PVA (white) glue, then with white acrylic primer.

5 Paint each shape with gouache paints, then decorate with gold paint and allow to dry.

6 Varnish with gloss and allow to dry. Suspend the smaller shapes from the hand using the jump rings. Suspend the larger shapes from three of the wire coils and hang these from the hand. Attach the remaining wire coils to the wings. Attach the small stars to the sun piece. Thread a length of picture wire through the two coils on the wings for hanging.

ASTRAL CLOCK

An impressive starburst clock with rays cut out of shining copper. The face is a simple disc of clay, painted in turquoise to give a verdigris effect.

YOU WILL NEED

MATERIALS
tracing paper
thin card or paper
0.5 mm copper sheet,
10 x 25 cm/4 x 10 in
modelling clay, 450 g/1 lb
acrylic paints: deep turquoise,
lemon-yellow and white
varnish
gold powder
epoxy resin glue
clock movement and hands

EQUIPMENT
pencil
metal cutters
sandpaper
rolling pin
clay-modelling tools
paintbrush

1 Trace the templates from the back of the book, enlarging if necessary, and cut out of card or paper. Draw the outlines for four large and four small rays on the copper sheet. Cut out with metal cutters and sand the edges.

2 Roll out the clay to a flat sheet 5 mm/¼ in thick.

3 Place the template on the clay and cut out the shape. Trace the inner circle with a modelling tool to impress the shape in the clay.

4 Roll a clay snake and place along the inner circle. Join the ends, then join it to the clockface and smooth with wet fingers. Make a hole in the middle of the face.

5 Press the short rays into the side of the clay and allow to dry completely.

6 Mix turquoise, yellow and white paint and paint the face of the clock.

7 Paint the clockface with a layer of varnish and allow to dry.

8 Mix the gold powder with varnish and decorate the ridge around the clock with thick gold lines.

9 Bend the bases of the long copper rays to fit over the edge of the face. Glue firmly in position with epoxy resin.

10 Fix the movement to the back of the clock and screw the hands on to the front.

ZODIAC MOBILE

An ethereal decoration inspired by a host of astrological signs. To achieve its balance, you will need to cut the wire for the various shapes to the exact lengths as given in the steps below.

YOU WILL NEED

MATERIALS
soft galvanized wire,
2 mm/0.078 in,
1.6 mm/0.062 in and
1 mm/0.039 in
medium-weight binding wire
tracing paper
paper
aerosol car paints: white
primer, midnight-blue and gold

EQUIPMENT
wire-cutters
round-nosed pliers
pencil
flat-nosed pliers

1 Use 2 mm/0.078 in wire for hangers: cut one 76 cm/ 30 in length and two 38 cm/ 15 in lengths. Make a loop in the centre of each. Secure with binding wire. Form waves and coils at each end using pliers. Trace the templates from the back of the book on to paper, enlarging as necessary.

4 For Sagittarius, cut two lengths of 1.6 mm/0.062 in wire, 25 cm/10 in. Bend into the bow shapes and bind ends together, trimming the excess. Make the bow string with binding wire.

7 Follow the templates for Taurus, Leo, Aries and Pisces, binding as shown in the main picture and trimming any excess. You need the following lengths: Taurus: 33 cm/13 in of 1.6 mm/0.062 in wire; the 1 cm/½ in diameter ring is made from the same wire. Leo: 38 cm/15 in of 1.6 mm/ 0.062 in wire; 20 cm/8 in of 1 mm/0.039 in wire for the crown. Aries: 102 cm/40 in of 1.6 mm/0.062 in wire. Pisces: 76 cm/30 in of 1.6 mm/0.062 in wire.

2 Carefully shape wire around the templates to form the motifs. For the scorpion's body, use 64 cm/26 in of 1.6 mm/0.062 in wire. Bind the ends at the head and trim. Cut two lengths of 1 mm/0.039 in wire, 33 cm/13 in, for claws. Shape, bind to the body and trim.

5 Bend a 56 cm/22 in length of 1 mm/0/039 in wire into an arrow shape, bind along the shaft and secure to the bow in the centre.

8 Spray paint the hangers and motifs with white primer and then paint them in the colours as shown.

3 Following the scorpion template, use binding wire for the back legs and the tail detail.

6 For Libra, cut 34 cm/ 13½ in of 2 mm/0.078 in wire. Bend into a bar shape, coiling the ends into loops. Bend the arms at the centre. For scales, cut two lengths of 1.6 mm/0.039 in wire, 23 cm/9 in. Bend into shape. Use binding wire to outline the dishes and bind to the bar.

9 Assemble the mobile by attaching the shapes to the hangers with nylon thread, as shown in the main picture.

GLOW IN THE DARK CLOCK

Read the time in the dark from this amusing clock made from special, luminous polymer clay.

YOU WILL NEED

MATERIALS

2¾ blocks glow-in-the-dark polymer clay
thin card
¼ block polymer clay: yellow, light and dark blue and light and dark green
jewellery wire
aluminium foil
jewellery head pins
epoxy resin glue
clock movement and hands

EQUIPMENT

rolling pin
craft knife
cutting mat
metal ruler
pencil
pair of compasses
film canister
smoothing tool
crosshead screw
dressmaker's pin
ballpoint pen
wire-cutters

1 Roll out the glow-in-the dark clay to 5 mm/¼ in thick. Cut a 10 x 13 cm/4 x 5 in rectangle. Cut a circular template and cut round to shape the top. Squeeze a film canister and stamp an oval near to the bottom.

2 Make templates for a slightly curved strip and for the oval cut out in step 1. Roll some yellow clay and cut out these shapes. Wrap the strip around the oval to form a tapered cup.

3 Fix the cup over the hole in the clockface. Smooth over the join. Mark the hours on the circular template and position on the back plate. Prick through the centre to mark the clockface. Stamp a hole for the clock spindle.

4 Cut out two strips of the rolled out glow-in-the dark clay to 3 cm/1¼ in wide. Make one 31 cm/12¼ in and the other 10 cm/4 in long. Use a narrow tube to stamp a small hole at the mid-point of the longer strip.

5 Assemble the strips to make the sides of the clockface, smoothing over the joins. Fix the sides to the back of the clockface and smooth over the joins.

6 Roll a marble-size piece of light blue clay into an egg shape. Crumble some dark blue clay and roll the egg in it to speckle the surface.

7 Put two short wires into the egg. Remove the wires and bake the egg in the oven following the manufacturer's instructions.

8 Cut a glow-in-the-dark clay rectangle to cover the bottom section of the back. Pack the cavity with foil. Bake the clockface.

9 Twist together some thin strips of yellow and light and dark green clay to create a marbled sausage.

10 Cut the sausage into one long and four short pieces. Join the pieces to make a central stem with four branches. Taper one end.

11 Make incisions along the branches and stem and insert wires long enough to protrude from the ends of the branches and the non-tapered stem end. Close up the slits and smooth over.

12 Roll out some yellow clay and form a three-petalled flower. Roll out some green clay and shape four leaves. Press patterns on the leaves and flower using the tip of a screw and a pen.

13 Push the flower and the leaves on to the wires of the stem and branches, and bake. When assembled, the tapered stem slots into the hole at the top of the clock.

14 Twist together thin strips of light and dark blue clay. Slice off 12 discs. Roll into balls and flatten. Stamp each with the end of a screw. Make a hole in the middle. Bake.

15 Push a jewellery head pin through each disc, dab a spot of glue on the back and push the pin into the clockface, at an hour marking. Allow to dry, then snip off the excess wire at the back. Hold the clock movement at the back of the clockface. Push the spindle through the hole from the front and screw together.

NIGHT AND DAY MOBILE

Golden suns and moody blue moons contrast with each other in this attractive mobile. Although mobiles are usually associated with children's rooms, this one is sophisticated enough to hang up as a decoration in any room in the house.

YOU WILL NEED

MATERIALS
corrugated card
newspaper
masking tape
wallpaper paste
small brass screw hooks
epoxy resin glue
PVA (white) glue
white undercoat paint
gouache paints: blue, silver, orange and gold
gloss and matt varnishes
gold enamel paint
small jewellery jump rings
picture-hanging wire

EQUIPMENT
pencil
craft knife
cutting mat
paintbrushes

1 Draw all the freehand shapes on the corrugated card and cut them out with a sharp craft knife.

2 Bulk out the shapes by scrunching up pieces of newspaper and wrapping masking tape around them to secure them in place.

3 Cover the pieces in several layers of newspaper strips soaked in wallpaper paste. Allow to dry overnight, or longer if necessary.

4 Screw in the hooks in the appropriate places for hanging, securing them with epoxy resin glue.

5 Coat the shapes with PVA (white) glue and allow to dry. Coat with white undercoat and allow to dry again.

6 Use gouache paints to decorate the shapes.

7 Give the shapes several coats of gloss varnish, picking out some areas in matt varnish to contrast. Allow to dry. Add details in gold enamel, painted on with a fine brush.

8 Assemble all the pieces, using the hooks and jump rings to join them together. Suspend the mobile from a length of picture wire threaded through the hook and ring in the topmost sun shape.

ASTROLOGICAL CLOCK

The passing of time is the real essence of astrology, as the stars make their regular courses around the heavens: you can reflect their progress with this stylish clock. Simple battery-run movements are now readily available: all you really have to supply is the clockface.

YOU WILL NEED

MATERIALS
sheet of thick white card
set of zodiac signs
PVA (white) glue
black acrylic paint
quartz clock movement and hands

EQUIPMENT
ruler
scissors
pair of compasses
pencil
craft knife
cutting mat
paintbrush

1 Cut a square of card measuring 20 cm/8 in. Draw a circle slightly smaller than the square. Cut out a small circle in the centre of the card to fit the clock spindle. Draw a set of zodiac symbols using the templates at the back of the book. Cut out.

2 Arrange the 12 star signs around the clockface, in the correct order (as shown in the picture). Position those corresponding to 12, 3, 6 and 9 o'clock first, then space the rest equally. Stick the zodiac symbols down with PVA (white) glue.

3 Paint the area around the clockface black. Allow the paint to dry, then seal the whole clock with two coats of diluted PVA (white) glue. Attach the clock movement to the back and fit the hands to the spindle. Insert a battery to complete.

GILDED TIMEPIECE

This clock, decorated with a découpaged print of an antique map of the heavens, combines practicality with a reminder of the timeless mystery of the stars. The luxurious gilded finish enhances the atmosphere created by the map; hang the clock where it will catch the light and create a mood of serenity and contemplation.

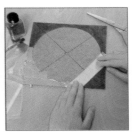

YOU WILL NEED

MATERIALS	EQUIPMENT
hardboard, 30 x 30 cm / 12 x 12 in	pencil
celestial map print	ruler
all-purpose glue	scissors
Japanese gold size	drill, with size 10 bit
Dutch gold leaf transfer book	paintbrush
clock movement and hands	

1 Using a pencil and ruler, draw two diagonals across the hardboard, to find the centre of the square. Cut out the celestial map and find its centre in the same way. Place the map on the hardboard, draw around the outside of the map, and remove it.

2 Drill a hole in the centre of the hardboard to fit the width of the clock mechanism. Paint a coat of size around the edge, up to the pencil line. Leave until touch-dry. Lay strips of gold leaf on top of the size to cover. Trim off any excess by rubbing with a finger.

3 Pierce a hole in the centre of the map for the hands. Stick the map in position.

4 Add the hands and the clock movement.

SEA CREATURES MOBILE

These creatures will be an instant hit with adults and children.

In order for the mobile to balance well, the shapes must be hung from the following lengths of thread: crab 14cm/5½in, dolphin 8 cm/3 in, seaweed 8 cm/3 in, seahorse 11 cm/4½in, large fish 12 cm/3¾in, shell 13 cm/5 in, small fish 8 cm/3 in, big starfish 8 cm/3 in, small starfish 8 cm/3 in.

YOU WILL NEED

MATERIALS
thick galvanized wire, 2 mm, 1.6 mm and 1.2 mm double-sided tape binding wire tracing paper thin card or paper aerosol car paints: red, yellow, aquamarine, blue and green nylon thread

EQUIPMENT
wire-cutters round-nosed pliers half-round jewellery pliers

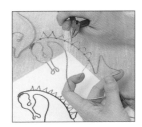

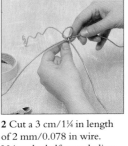

1 To make the small supports, cut two 45 cm/18 in lengths of 2 mm/0.078 in wire. Bend each wire into an arch and form a coil at each end, using round-nosed pliers. Bend a curve in the wire, beside each coil, using half-round pliers. Make two main supports in the same way from 74 cm/29 in lengths of 2 mm/0.078 in wire. Bend waves in the wire, beside coils.

2 Cut a 3 cm/1¼ in length of 2 mm/0.078 in wire. Using the half-round pliers, bend the wire round, to make a ring. Cross the main support wires, so that they meet exactly in the centre and tape them together, with the ring at the top, using double-sided tape. Wrap the binding wire around the join, to secure it, covering the double-sided tape.

3 Trace the templates from the back of the book, enlarging them to 300%. Form each creature by shaping the wire around the template. First, cut a 90 cm/35½ in length of 1.6 mm/0.062 in wire. Form it into a seaweed shape, following the template from the book. Join the ends together and wrap them with binding wire.

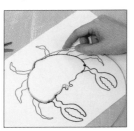

4 Following the template, form the crab's body from a 40 cm/16 in length of 1.6 mm/0.062 in wire. Make an eye loop at each end of the wire.

5 Make the front legs from two 29 cm/11½ in lengths of 1.2 mm/0.047 in wire. Twist the ends of the legs around the crab's body and secure.

6 Use a continuous length of binding wire to make the back legs. Wrap the wire around the crab's body, between the legs.

7 Using 1.6 mm/0.062 in wire, make: a shell from 22 cm/8½ in, two starfish from 32 cm/12½ in and 50 cm/19½ in, and a seahorse from 97 cm/38 in. Join and wrap the ends with binding

wire. Use binding wire to make fins, nipping a point in each arch. Make a small fish from 71 cm/28 in wire, and a large fish from 100 cm/40 in wire. On the large fish, curve the wire across the

back. Give each fish a wavy line of wire between head and body, binding the joins. Bend 108 cm/42½ in wire around the dolphin outline. Bind the joins.

8 Spray paint the sea creatures in one or two colours. To assemble, follow the finished picture. Attach the sea creatures to the supports with nylon thread.

TEAPOT CLOCK

*Salt dough is easy to prepare and it is so versatile
that almost any shape can be sculpted from it.
Children, in particular, enjoy working with
the medium.*

YOU WILL NEED

MATERIALS
*aluminium foil
325 g/8 oz/2¾ cups flour
325 g/8 oz/2¾ cups salt
2 tbsp vegetable oil
200 ml/8 fl oz/1 cup water
baking parchment
florist's wire
acrylic paints: cream and blue
clear acrylic varnish
clock movement and hands*

EQUIPMENT
*small ovenproof plate
mixing bowl
rolling pin
trefoil-shape cutter
skewer
baking tray
scissors
paintbrushes*

1 Turn the plate over and cover the underside with aluminium foil, padding out the centre, if necessary, so it is slightly raised.

2 Mix together the flour, salt, oil and water to form the dough. Knead thoroughly and roll out a circle slightly larger than the plate. Lay over the foil, cut a circle in the centre for the spindle and trim to size.

3 Roll sausage shapes for the lid, trim and base. Dampen both dough surfaces before positioning the pieces and press them firmly in place.

4 Shape and add the spout. Mark the flower design with a trefoil cutter and the end of a skewer. Each flower represents a numeral. Prick a dot pattern along the lid and the base.

5 Place on a tray covered in baking parchment and bake for at least five hours at 110°C/225°F/Gas ¼. After one hour take out of the oven and allow to cool. Bend some florist's wire into a handle shape and cover with dough. Fix to the body clock.

6 Return to the oven for about four hours. Allow to cool, then carefully remove the plate. Paint the clock in cream and allow to dry. Paint the flowers pale blue and pick out the details in dark blue.

7 Cover with several coats of clear varnish, allowing it to dry between coats. Fit the clock movement and hands.

WIRE SUNFLOWER MOBILE

This mobile has a really light and airy feel. Wire can be bent into a variety of interesting and attractive shapes with pliers, and these sunflowers have the pleasing simplicity of a child's drawing. This would make a lovely decoration for a child's room or for any sunny corner.

YOU WILL NEED

MATERIALS	EQUIPMENT
thick aluminium wire, 2 mm/0.078 in, 1.6 mm/0.062 in and 1 mm/0.039 in binding wire	wire-cutters
	long ruler
	3 round containers, about
tracing paper	6.5 cm/2½ in, 5 cm/2 in and
paper	2.5 cm/1 in diameter
aerosol car paints: white	indelible magic marker
primer, yellow, brown and green	flat-nosed pliers
masking tape	round-nosed pliers
strong green thread	pencil
strong clear glue	scissors

1 Cut lengths of wire for the struts and flowers: large strut, 59 cm/23½ in of 2 mm/0.078 in wire; short ones 2 x 38 cm/15 in of 2 mm/0.078 in wire; small ring, 2 cm/¾ in of 2 mm/0.078 in wire; large flower, 104 cm/42 in of 1.6 mm/0.062 in wire; centre circle of large flower, 7 cm/2¾ in of 2 mm/0.078 in wire; medium-size flowers with stems, 2 x 145 cm/57 in of 1.6 mm/0.062 in wire; centre circles of flowers, 2 x 5.5 cm/2¼ in of 2 mm/0.078 in wire; small flowers, 5 x 42 cm/16½ in of 1 mm/0.039 in wire; centre circles of small flowers, 5 x 3 cm/1¼ in of 1.6 mm/0.062 in wire.

2 Bend the wires for the centres of all the flowers around circular containers that are slightly smaller than the centres.

3 For the large flower, mark along the wire with a magic marker 2 cm/¾ in from one end and then at ten intervals of 10 cm/4 in.

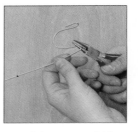

4 Bend the wire into folds at every mark.

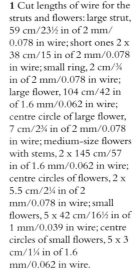

5 Pinch each of the folds together tightly with the flat-nosed pliers.

6 Using round-nosed pliers, bend the centre peaks and curve the petals into shape. Snip off the ends, leaving a small hook for binding the flower to its centre.

7 Bind in the centre circle with binding wire, folding the binding wire over each loop and twisting it tightly, to secure it. Repeat the process for the small flowers, marking the wire at 1 cm/½ in from the end and at ten intervals of 4 cm/1½ in.

8 For the medium-size flowers with stems, mark 35 cm/13¾ in from the end and at ten intervals of 8 cm/3 in apart, leaving another end of 36 cm/14 in. Fold the petals as for the large flower. Use the remaining wire to form the leaves.

9 Bind the two stem wires together, using binding wire, to secure the leaves at the base. Bind the centre circle as in step 6. Bend the wires for the struts, using the templates at the back of the book as a guide. Spray everything with white primer. Allow to dry. Spray the pieces in the appropriate colours, masking off any areas as necessary, and leaving to dry between colours. Make up the mobile, securing the threads to the pieces with a knot and a spot of glue.

TEX MEX CLOCK

Add a touch of the Wild West to your home with this cheerful "cowboy" wall clock. You can obtain the clock mechanism and hands from craft shops. If you prefer, you could make the clock circular, or even square, and arrange the motifs differently.

YOU WILL NEED

MATERIALS	EQUIPMENT
tracing paper	pencil
thin card	scissors
2 quantities of salt dough (see page 136)	rolling pin
	craft knife
baking parchment	cutting mat
16 silver star studs	dressmaker's pin
acrylic or craft paints	baking tray
silver craft paint	paintbrushes
polyurethane matt varnish	
clock movement and hands	

1 Trace the templates from the back of the book, transfer to card and cut out the shapes. Roll the dough out to 1 cm/½ in thick. Place the clock template on top and cut around the outer edge. Push a pin through the template into the clock at the dots to mark the positions of the hours and the clock centre. Remove the template. Insert the star studs at the hour points and along the lower edge.

2 Cut a hole at the centre for the clockwork spoke to be inserted through it and add an extra 3 mm/⅛ in to the diameter of the hole to allow for painting and varnishing. Roll out the remaining dough on baking parchment to 5 mm/¼ in thick. Use the templates to cut four cacti and a pair of cowboy boots, cutting the boot straps and spurs separately. Pat the cut edges of the piece with a moistened finger. Indent the details with the tip of a knife.

3 Moisten the cowboy boots and place the straps and spurs in place. Emboss a "stud" on each spur with the head of a pin. Place all the pieces on a baking tray and bake for one hour at 110°C/225°F/Gas ¼. Moisten the undersides of the cacti and cowboy boots. Smear sparingly with dough and press in position on the clock.

4 Bake for a further nine hours. Allow to cool, then paint the clock. Use a fine brush to paint the stitching on the boots and paint the clock hands and details with silver paint. Apply five coats of varnish. Assemble the clock movement and hands.

CELESTIAL MOBILE

Stars, the crescent moon and a huge shooting star jostle each other in this amusing mobile. The little star-shaped cut-outs in the meteor's tail can all be joined by saw cuts, so you need drill only one hole through which to pass the saw blade.

YOU WILL NEED

MATERIALS	EQUIPMENT
tracing paper	pencil
5 mm /¼ in birch plywood	fretsaw
white undercoat paint	drill
chrome finish spray paint	sandpaper
acrylic paints	paintbrushes
varnish	
fine nylon fishing line	

1 Trace the templates from the back of the book, enlarging if necessary, and transfer to the plywood. Cut them out.

2 Drill a small hole inside the circle of the shooting star and through the first cut-out in the tail. Pass the saw blade through each of these to make the internal cuts. With a very small bit, drill holes through the top of each piece and in the marked positions on the hanger. Lightly sand all the pieces.

3 Paint all the pieces with undercoat. Allow to dry, then spray the top of the shooting star and the crescent moon with chrome paint. Complete the decoration using acrylic paints and varnish.

4 Tie the stars to the hanger with thin nylon line. Make sure they do not bump into each other. Add a loop of nylon to the hole at the top.

SUNBURST CLOCK

This luxurious clock takes its inspiration from the styles that were favoured by Louis XIV, the Sun King.

YOU WILL NEED

MATERIALS
tracing paper
bronze-coloured velvet,
36 x 36 cm/14 x 14 in
2 pieces of metallic organza in
dark gold and cream,
36 x 36 cm/14 x 14 in
tacking (basting) thread
sewing machine
machine embroidery threads:
gold and black
mounting board
fabric glue
clock movement and hands

EQUIPMENT
pencil
tape measure
dressmaker's pins
needle
dressmaker's scissors
pair of compasses
craft knife
cutting mat
paintbrush

1 Trace the template from the back of the book, enlarging to a diameter of 30 cm/12 in. Lay the dark gold, then the cream organza on top of the velvet. Pin the template in the centre and tack (baste) in place.

2 Using gold thread and the widest setting, satin stitch around the outer circle of the sun, joining all the layers of fabric together. Outline the main facial outline, the nostrils and the areas under the eyes in medium satin stitch with gold.

3 Using black thread and a single line of medium satin stitch, outline all the other features, apart from the upper mouth and eyebrows as these need a double line.

4 Outline the inner circle in black thread on the widest satin stitch setting. Change the setting to medium and outline the sun's rays.

5 Unpick the tacking (basting) and cut away the loose threads. Cut away the tracing paper.

6 Following the main picture, cut away one or two layers of the fabric to reveal the colours beneath.

7 Using a pair of compasses, draw a circle 30 cm/12 in in diameter on mounting board, and cut out.

8 Stick the fabric cloth on to the board with fabric glue.

9 Cut a hole through the centre of the clockface. Push through the clock movement and attach the hands.

PAPIER-MACHE MOBILE

This colourful mobile is made from papier-mâché, elaborately painted with gouache colours. The more individual you make the decoration, the more charming it becomes.

YOU WILL NEED

MATERIALS
newspaper
masking tape
tracing paper
corrugated card
wallpaper paste
screw eyes
epoxy resin glue
chemical metal filler
mirror fragments
PVA (white) glue
white acrylic primer
gouache paints
gloss varnish
gold enamel paint
galvanized wire
jewellery jump rings

EQUIPMENT
pencil
scissors
craft knife
cutting mat
small and fine paintbrushes
paint-mixing container
wire-cutters
round-nosed pliers

1 Roll up some newspaper, bend it in the centre and then bend the ends over, to make a heart shape. Secure the ends with masking tape. Trace the template for the wings and stars from the back of the book, enlarging if necessary, and cut them out from corrugated card. Cut two slits in the side of the biggest heart, slot in the wings, and secure with tape.

2 Tear more newspaper into strips. Cover all the hearts and stars with several layers of newspaper strips, each one dipped in wallpaper paste. Allow to dry.

3 Screw small screw eyes in place, securing them with epoxy glue. Allow to dry. Then mix up the filler, according to the manufacturer's instructions. Spread filler on the wings and carefully push in pieces of broken mirror. Allow to dry. Repeat the process on the back of the wings.

4 Coat all the shapes (except the wings) in PVA (white) glue and allow to dry. Paint on a layer of white acrylic primer, using a fine brush to fill between the mirror pieces.

5 Paint on the design using gouache paints.

6 Coat with several layers of gloss varnish. When dry, add detail in gold enamel.

7 Cut a 40 cm/16 in length of wire and two lengths of 28 cm/11 in. Using round-nosed pliers, coil the wire into shape, following the template outlines. Coat in turn with white glue, primer, and gold enamel, allowing each coat to dry before applying the next.

8 Assemble the mobile using small jump rings and round-nosed pliers.

DECORATIVE BOXES

Boxes range in sizes and shapes, but the projects in this section all have one thing in common – they show you how to transform an otherwise plain object into something very special. Whether you choose to make a storage box or a small confetti box, you are bound to enjoy the processes involved. So take a look around your home and find a box that's just crying out for some decoration, then choose a project from this section and give it a whole new look that pleases you and suits your home.

MATERIALS AND EQUIPMENT

Materials

White undercoat for unpainted wood surfaces.

Matt emulsion (flat latex) paint in various colours. Don't feel bound to use the colours suggested for each project: you can always choose tones to suit your own colour scheme.

A selection of artist's acrylic or stencil paints for stencilled motifs, patterns and detailing.

Clear, water-based varnish
PVA (white) glue

Equipment

Medium-sized household paint-brushes (at least two).
Stencil brush
Selection of artist's brushes (including a long-haired brush).
Selection of paint pots and paint trays
A cloth
Masking tape
Spray adhesive
Acetate sheet or waxy stencil card To make stencils.
Craft knife or sharp scissors For cutting stencils.
Medium and fine-grade sandpaper
Fine-grade steel wool For rubbing down paint to give a worn or "distressed" look.

Of all household objects, boxes are the simplest and most universal – and the easiest to decorate. In the days of folk art, in Europe and in colonial America, boxes were the most common form of painted object, made in many sizes for every type of household storage and transportation.

Traditional boxes along these lines included the church box, carried to Sunday services by women to hold their Bibles and gloves, and the bride's box, given on the wedding day and decorated with a painting of the bride, and sometimes of the groom, the date of the marriage and the bride's initials.

Such a rich history provides a wealth of traditional decorative motifs and approaches that can be used to create highly

personalized gifts or simple household accessories with real colour and character.

The projects in this section offer a marvellous range of possibilities – including not only wooden boxes, but also highly decorative and colourful examples made of papier-mâché, thick cardboard, even salt dough.

Each project tells you what you will need in the way of equipment and materials. When working with wood, however, you are likely to need some or all of the following:

ABOVE *A modern blanket chest painted in imitation of a traditional Scandinavian bridal chest.*

RIGHT *A nineteenth-century painted marriage box from Norway.*

148

MATERIALS AND EQUIPMENT

ABOVE *A range of country-style paints in traditional colours – but feel free to match colours to your own interior scheme.*

Preparing wood surfaces for painting

If a wooden box is thickly painted or varnished, use paint stripper (or have the object dipped). If existing paint is in reasonable condition, simply sand it down and apply a base coat. On new wood, sand surfaces with medium sandpaper, apply white undercoat, and allow to dry. When undercoat is dry, sand again with fine sandpaper.

Découpage

For those with less confidence in their painting skills, one of the most effective methods of decorating boxes is découpage. This technique works as well for cardboard boxes as for wood – and allows you great control over the end result. Pretty coloured images and patterns cut out and stuck down can be given several coats of water-based gloss varnish to make them sparkle.

Alternatively, you can photocopy black-and-white images and glue them on to boxes to make striking designs.

Multimedia

Quite a few of the box projects in this section combine a variety of techniques such as painting, gilding and stamping – making these projects a great way of practising a range of craft skills on a relatively small scale.

ABOVE *This painted box, treated in detail later in the section, shows how easy it is to get a rustic "look" to a piece by using the folk art templates in the back of the book.*

RIGHT AND BELOW *Steps toward achieving the finished effect.*

SEAHORSE STORAGE BOX

Delicate, swirling brushstrokes create a watery background for this delightful seahorse. The box could be used for storing stationery, pencils, jewellery or even cosmetics.

YOU WILL NEED

MATERIALS
5 mm/¼ in thick pine slat, 68 cm/26½ in long and 3 cm/1¼ in wide wood glue masking tape 5 mm/¼ in thick birch-faced plywood sheet, 40 x 40 cm/16 x 16 in white undercoat paint acrylic paints: blue, white, green and gold tracing paper stencil card or acetate sheet

EQUIPMENT
ruler coping saw or fretsaw medium and fine-grade sandpaper pencil paintbrush craft knife cutting mat stencil brush

1 Cut two 20 cm/8 in and two 14 cm/5½ in lengths of pine with a saw. Sand the rough edges and glue the pieces together to form the sides of the box. Hold the frame together with masking tape while the glue is drying.

2 Place the frame on the plywood and draw around the inside, to mark out the base of the box. Cut out the base. Repeat the process to make the lid insert. Draw around the outside of the box and cut out to make the lid. Glue the base into the frame. Sand around the lid insert and make sure that it will fit in the box, before gluing it to the lid.

3 Sand the box and then apply a coat of white undercoat paint.

4 When dry, sand the box again, using fine sandpaper. Using two shades of blue acrylic, paint the box with swirling brushstrokes.

5 Trace the template from the back of the book, enlarging if necessary. Transfer it to stencil card or acetate and cut it out.

6 Tape the stencil on to the lid to hold it firmly in place. Stencil the pattern, using a combination of blue and green acrylics. Finish with a light smattering of gold. When the paint is dry, lightly sand the whole box with fine sandpaper.

CREPE PAPER GIFT BOX

To make a gift seem even more special, present it in this decorated box. The romantic roses make it perfect for a wedding present.

YOU WILL NEED

MATERIALS	EQUIPMENT
single- and double-sided crepe paper in soft colours	*scissors*
adhesive tape	*ruler*
round card box, with lid	*glue gun and glue sticks*
wire-edged ribbon	

1 To make a rose, cut through folded crepe paper to make two strips about 5 cm/2 in wide. Tape two strips at right angles to each other. Fold one over the other to make a concertina. Continue in this fashion until the end of the strip.

2 Holding the ends, stretch the concertina to its fullest extent and wind it up, twisting to get a rose shape. Tape the ends of the strips into a "stalk". Make several roses of different colours and sizes.

3 Cover the box and lid with crepe paper, neatly pleating the fullness and sticking it down so it is as flat as possible in the centre of the lid.

4 Glue the roses on top and finish with a ribbon.

CONFETTI BOX

This sweet little paper box makes a much prettier holder for confetti than a shop-bought one, and can be kept long after the wedding is over as a reminder of a special day.

YOU WILL NEED

MATERIALS	EQUIPMENT
tracing paper	*pencil*
stiff paper or card	*scissors*
pink paint	*paintbrush*
gold ink	*ruler*
double-sided adhesive tape	*blunt knife*
ribbon	*craft knife*
rose-petal confetti	*cutting mat*

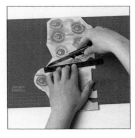

1 Trace the template from the back of the book on to card, enlarging if necessary. Draw around it and cut it out. Wet the card and paint rough pink shapes, so that the colour bleeds out. Dry. With gold ink, paint circles and leaf shapes. Allow to dry.

2 With a ruler and blunt knife, score the fold lines.

3 With a craft knife, cut the slits for the ribbon.

4 Cut a piece of double-sided tape and stick it to one side of the tab. Peel off the backing, overlap the tab and stick in place. Fold under the bottom edge and thread the ribbon through the slits. Fill with rose confetti and then tie the ribbon in a bow.

FOLK ART BOX

The cupid motif is very popular in traditional folk art designs. Here, it has been used to embellish an oval Shaker-style box. The distressed hand-painted finish gives it a timeless quality that will ensure it is treasured for ever.

YOU WILL NEED

MATERIALS
oval card box
corrugated card
PVA (white) glue
newspaper
wallpaper paste
white acrylic primer
acrylic paints: dark green,
brick-red, yellow-ochre,
pale blue and brown

EQUIPMENT
craft knife
cutting mat
paintbrushes
paint-mixing container
sandpaper

1 Trace the templates from the back of the book, enlarging them to fit the lid of your box. Trace the shapes on to the card, cut them out and glue them to the lid of the box.

2 Soak small strips of newspaper in wallpaper paste. Stick three layers over the edges of the card shapes. Allow to dry. Paint the lid and box with white acrylic primer. Allow to dry.

3 Paint the box and the background of the lid with a coat of dark green. When it is dry, paint with brick-red and allow to dry. Sand down for a distressed finish.

4 Paint the cupid, mixing the colours to create subtle shades. Use a fine paintbrush for the border and the decoration. Stipple the cheeks with a dry brush.

DECOUPAGE OAK LEAF BOX

Find one pretty motif and you can create lovely repeat patterns with it instantly, using a photocopier. Copies of old engravings are perfect for this technique: here they were delicately hand-coloured in a selection of autumnal shades.

YOU WILL NEED

MATERIALS
*wooden box
cream emulsion (latex) paint
black and white leaf motif
acrylic paints: yellow-ochre and
red oxide
PVA (white) glue
clear gloss acrylic varnish*

EQUIPMENT
*paintbrushes
paint-mixing container
scissors
craft knife
cutting mat*

1 Paint the box with two or three coats of cream paint. Make copies of the leaf motif in two sizes for the sides and lid. Hand-tint the copies with a thin wash of yellow-ochre and then red oxide.

2 Use scissors to cut around the outside of the leaf shapes. Cut away any small spaces within the design with a craft knife.

3 Arrange the leaves on the lid and sides of the box. Glue them on with PVA (white) glue and allow to dry.

4 Protect the box with two or three coats of clear gloss varnish. Allow the varnish to dry thoroughly between each coat.

SUN HATBOX

This hatbox positively glitters with gold decoration, creating an effect that seems to glow like the heavenly bodies to which it pays tribute.

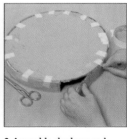

YOU WILL NEED

MATERIALS	EQUIPMENT
carpet roll tube	*saw (optional)*
card	*tape measure*
masking tape	*pair of compasses*
newspaper strips	*pencil*
PVA (white) glue	*ruler*
white undercoat paint	*craft knife*
acrylic paints: blue, deep violet	*paintbrushes*
and red	*scissors*
gold paint	
sun-face motif print	
glitter glue	

1 Using a section of a carpet tube, cut with a saw for the cylindrical part of the box, or bend a piece of card into a cylinder. Draw and cut a circle of card for the base and another slightly larger circle for the lid.

2 To make the lid, cut a long narrow strip of card the length of the circumference of the lid, plus a small overlap. Bend the strip and fix it in position with masking tape. Bind the edge and the join with strips of newspaper and slightly watered–down PVA (white) glue.

3 Assemble the base and sides, fix with masking tape and bind the edge and joins with newspaper strips in the same way as the lid. Allow to dry.

4 Prime the base and lid with white undercoat paint.

5 Mark the stripes on the side of the box and paint them in different colours. Allow to dry. Use gold paint to add fine stripes.

6 Paint the details with gold paint and a fine brush.

7 Paint the lid violet. Photocopy the motif about 18 times. Cut the motifs out and stick them to the lid and the side of the box, using plenty of watered–down PVA (white) glue.

8 Paint the faces of the motifs to highlight all the features. Add glitter glue squiggles to fill any gaps.

BUG BOX

If you have access to a photocopier you can make up striking and original designs on paper. Before you begin this project, it's a good idea to measure your box carefully and keep a note of all the dimensions to be sure that your design will fit well.

YOU WILL NEED

MATERIALS
insect images
white A3 (tabloid) paper
glue stick
shoe box
white acrylic or poster paint
PVA (white) glue
black paper
clear matt varnish

EQUIPMENT
scissors
paintbrush

1 Photocopy the images to the desired size. Arrange them on A3 paper and secure in place with a glue stick. When you are happy with your arrangement, make enough copies of it to cover the box, plus a few spares in case you go wrong. Two designs have been used here: one with a large central motif for the top of the box, and the other with insects scattered all over the paper.

2 Paint the box with white paint and allow to dry. Brush a thin layer of PVA (white) glue over the top and sides of the lid. Position your covering paper carefully and smooth out from the centre to exclude air bubbles.

3 Make a straight cut to each corner of the lid top and trim the overlap at the corners and edges to 2 cm/¾ in. Smooth the paper over the sides, gluing each flap under the next side piece to make neat corners, and tucking the overlap inside the lid.

4 Measure the sides of the box, adding 2 cm/¾ in to each dimension, and cut four pieces of paper. Glue and cover the inner sides.

5 From the paper you used for the lid, cut the lining for the bottom to the exact size of the box and glue in place.

6 Cut a rectangle from the black paper large enough to cover the bottom and sides of the box with a 2 cm/¾ in overlap all round. Cut out a wavy edge 1 cm/¼ in deep. Make straight cuts to the corners of the box and trim the flaps, as before. Glue the paper to the box, turning in the edge.

7 Measure the inside of the box lid and cut a piece of black paper to fit, again allowing a 2 cm/¾ in overlap. Cut the wavy edge, trim the corners as before and glue.

8 Dilute some PVA (white) glue with water and brush all over the box and lid. This will go on cloudy but will clear as it dries. Finally, seal the box with a thick coat of varnish.

Valentine Box

A romantic gift for Valentine's Day, or any time of year. The combination of cut-out flowers and gold hearts creates a really strong, graphic impression, quite different from the usual whimsical "Victoriana" look. Découpage is an easy technique that gives truly spectacular results, making it possible to cover relatively large areas with a repeat pattern.

You Will Need

Materials
plain wooden box
red emulsion (latex) paint
floral wrapping paper
tracing paper
thin card
gold paper
glue
antique oak varnish
polyurethane varnish

Equipment
paintbrushes
scissors
pencil
cloth

1 Paint the box red inside and out. Cut out flower images of various sizes from the paper. Draw a freehand heart on card and cut around it. Place the heart template on the gold paper. Draw around it. Repeat seven times and cut out the gold hearts.

2 Arrange the hearts on the box, two on the lid and on each long side and one on each end. Glue in place. Position the flowers around the hearts and glue them, pushing out any air bubbles. Allow to dry.

3 Add a coat of antique varnish, and rub it off with a cloth, to give an old, soft look. Finish with three or four coats of polyurethane varnish, letting each one dry before adding the next one.

DANCING BEES BOX

The bees encircling this painted box have been cut out of folded paper like a row of dancing dolls. Measure the lid before you begin and enlarge or reduce the template so that the ring of bees will fit well. This box would make a wonderful gift filled with pots of honey or some beeswax cosmetics.

YOU WILL NEED

MATERIALS
tracing paper
thin card
circular painted box
black paper
yellow acrylic paint
all-purpose glue
clear varnish

EQUIPMENT
pencil
craft knife
cutting mat
white marker pencil
scissors
paintbrushes

1 Trace the template from the back of the book, enlarging to fit your box. Transfer to card and cut out. Fold some black paper in half, then in half again. Position the template across the folded corner so the tips of the wings touch the folds, and draw around it with a white pencil.

2 Cut out, making sure that the bees are joined by their wings. Unfold the bees carefully. Make two sets. Draw the bees' stripes on each circle and paint their stripes and wings in yellow acrylic paint.

3 Glue the bees to the lid of the box. Cut the second set in half and stick them on the sides of the box. Protect the box with a coat of varnish.

DRAGONFLY PRINT BOX

The background of this bold dragonfly print has been roughly cut to give it the look of a primitive woodcut. If you haven't tried lino-cutting before, practise on a scrap. Make sure the tools are very sharp and always keep your free hand out of the way of the cutting edge. Don't dig too deep.

YOU WILL NEED

MATERIALS
tracing paper
thick yellow paper
water-based block printing
paints: red, green and black
lino tile
PVA (white) glue
wooden box
clear varnish

EQUIPMENT
pencil
paintbrushes
lino cutters
craft knife
cutting mat
glass sheet
lino roller

1 Trace the template from the back of the book, enlarging if necessary. Transfer to yellow paper and paint in red and green. Trace the completed dragonfly motifs, turn the tracing over and transfer to the lino, giving a reverse image.

2 Cut out the design on the lino, cutting a criss-cross pattern freehand on the wings to give a lacy effect. Cut out the background roughly, leaving some areas untouched to give texture to the design. Trim the lino round the design to make positioning easier.

3 Spread the black paint on the glass sheet with the roller and roll it evenly on to the lino cut. Position the lino cut carefully on the paper and apply even pressure to make the print. Leave the print to dry, then glue it to the top of the box. Seal with a coat of varnish.

SWAN BOX

The stately swan, with its many regal associations, has long been used for decoration. The long and graceful neck of this heraldic bird is often adorned with the noble insignia of a coronet. This medieval patterned box is decorated with a dignified white swan standing against an ornate blue background.

YOU WILL NEED

MATERIALS
hexagonal box, with lid
acrylic gesso
tracing paper
thin card
craft paints: mid-blue, dark blue, white, black and orange
gold and silver paints
matt acrylic varnish

EQUIPMENT
paintbrushes
pencil
scissors
ruler
coarse-grade sandpaper

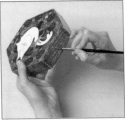

1 Prime the box with gesso. Trace the template from the back of the book. Transfer to thin card and cut out. Draw around it on to the lid. Rule a grid of 2 cm/¾ in squares over the background. Paint alternately in mid and dark blue. Paint the swan white, adding black details on the head and wing. Paint the coronet, feet and beak orange and add gold to the coronet.

2 Paint the lid edges and box sides in two shades of blue. When dry, rub very lightly over the whole box with some sandpaper to give a distressed look.

3 Paint silver diamonds over the corners of the background squares and add a tiny gold dot at each corner. Paint gold stars around the edges of the lid. Seal the box with several coats of varnish.

TOY BOX

This project gives instant appeal to the most ordinary of wooden boxes. It works just as well on old as new woods, but if you are using an old box, give it a good rub down with sandpaper first.

YOU WILL NEED

MATERIALS
hinged wooden box or chest, with lid
rust-red emulsion (latex) paint
emulsion (latex) or acrylic paints: maroon, sap-green, bright green and dark blue
small, large and trellis heart stamps
matt varnish

EQUIPMENT
paintbrushes
plate
foam roller
fine-grade sandpaper

1 Paint the box with rust-red paint, applying at least two coats to give a good matt background. Allow to dry between coats.

2 Run the roller through a plate of maroon paint until it is evenly coated. Use the roller to apply a border around the edge of the lid and allow to dry.

3 Spread some sap-green paint on to another plate and coat the roller. Ink the small stamp and print a few hearts randomly over the lid.

4 Ink the large and trellis stamps with sap-green paint. Print some hearts close together and others on their own to create a random pattern. Cover the whole lid in this way.

5 Clean all three stamps and ink with the bright green paint. Build up the pattern by adding this colour in the gaps, leaving enough space for the last two colours.

6 Using the dark blue paint, continue stamping the three hearts over the lid.

7 Fill in the remaining background space with maroon paint and the three heart stamps. No large spaces should remain. Allow to dry.

8 Use sandpaper to rub down the lid where you think natural wear and tear would occur.

9 You can preserve the comfortable "weathered" look of the toy box by applying two coats of matt varnish.

LEAF BOX

Keep this sturdy little box on your desk to hold bits and pieces, or make it to hold a memorable gift for someone special.

YOU WILL NEED

MATERIALS
pine slat,
8 x 45 mm / ⅛ x 1¼ in
wood glue
masking tape
5 mm / ¼ in birch-faced
plywood sheet
white undercoat paint
acrylic paints: bright yellow
and dark and light green
clear gloss acrylic varnish

EQUIPMENT
ruler
fretsaw
sandpaper
pencil
paintbrushes
paint-mixing container

1 Cut four equal lengths of pine slat and sand the rough edges. Glue to form the sides of the box, holding in place with masking tape. Draw a leaf shape freehand on to plywood. Cut out and sand around the edges.

2 Draw around the inside and outside of the box on to the plywood for the lid insert, lid and base. Cut out and sand. Glue in the base. Sand the insert to fit and glue to the lid. Sand all around the box.

3 Paint the box and leaf shape with two coats of undercoat. Sand between coats. When dry, draw the triangles and border on the sides and lid.

4 Paint the box yellow and the border and triangles green. Finish with varnish. Paint the leaf and varnish. Glue the leaf to the lid.

CANCER CRAB BOX

This attractive little box would make a delightful present in itself, or could contain an extra-special gift. The lid is painted in a wavy pattern inspired by the crab's watery home, but dotted with stars to underline its astrological significance.

YOU WILL NEED

MATERIALS

pine slats,
8 x 32 mm / 3/8 x 1¼ in, cut
into 4 x 10 cm / 4 in lengths
5 mm / ¼ in birch
plywood sheet, cut into the
following sizes:
base and lid insert:
8 x 10 cm / 3¼ x 4 in
lid: 11.5 x 10 cm / 4½ x 4 in
crab motif:
10 x 10 cm / 4 x 4 in
tracing paper
wood glue
masking tape
white undercoat paint
acrylic paints: deep cobalt,
deep yellow, cadmium-red,
gold, raw umber and black
matt varnish

EQUIPMENT

fretsaw
pencil
sandpaper
paintbrushes

1 Cut out the four pine slats and a base, lid and lid insert from the plywood. Trace the template from the back of the book, enlarging if necessary and transfer to the plywood. Cut out and sand off any rough edges.

2 Assemble the sides of the box with wood glue and hold in place with masking tape until the glue is dry. Glue in the base. Glue the lid insert centrally on the lid. Sand down any rough corners and edges.

3 Paint the box and crab with white undercoat. Sand lightly when dry. Paint the box and lid with the blue base colour applied with a wavy brushstroke. Paint on the border pattern and stars. Paint the crab in red, picking out details in blue and gold. Finish with a coat of matt varnish. Glue the crab firmly on to the lid.

BUSY BEE WORKBOX

You'll find any number of uses for this handy box. The stylized fretwork bee – the symbol of industry – is both decorative and functional, as it forms the handle of the box.

YOU WILL NEED

MATERIALS
*8 mm/⅜ in pine slat,
2 m x 7 cm/6 ft 6 in x 2¾ in
wood glue
tracing paper
carbon paper
5 mm/¼ in birch plywood,
38 x 20 cm/15 x 8 in
panel pins (optional)
light oak wood stain
polyurethane varnish
self-adhesive baize,
38 x 19 cm/15 x 7½ in*

EQUIPMENT
*tenon saw
pencil
5 mm/¼ in drill
fretsaw
sandpaper
hammer (optional)
paintbrush
fine wire wool
scissors*

1 Cut two 38 cm/15 in lengths of pine. Glue the two pieces together to form a single piece.

2 Trace the template from the back of the book, enlarging if necessary, and transfer to the centre of the board using carbon paper.

3 Drill a hole through each section of the bee. Pass the saw blade through each hole and saw out the design. Mark and saw the curve of the handle, making the ends 6.5 cm/2½ in deep. Sand.

4 Cut two 39.8 cm/15¾ in and two 20 cm/8 in lengths of pine for the sides of the box. Glue these around the plywood base. You may find it easier to fix the corners with panel pins while the glue dries.

5 Glue the handle section in place. Colour the box with wood stain and allow to dry, then varnish it.

6 Rub the box down with wire wool to achieve a warm lustre. Cut the baize in half and trim to fit in the base.

FLEUR-DE-LYS BOX

This design makes the most of the bold colours and geometric patterns of heraldry. The crunchy textures of the materials used are as eye-catching as the brilliant colours.

YOU WILL NEED

MATERIALS
*fusible bonding web,
13 x 13 cm/5 x 5 in
calico,
25 x 25 cm/10 x 10 in
1 cm/½ in wide corded
ribbon, 1 m/1 yd each of red
and green
bright yellow felt
embroidery threads: black
and yellow
tracing paper
gold bullion, size 2:
38 cm/15 in each of rough
and smooth
gold metallic embroidery thread
dark oak trinket box with lid
for 10 cm/4 in padded insert*

EQUIPMENT
*iron
cork board
scissors
dressmaker's pins
sewing machine
embroidery hoop
needle
large-eyed needle*

1 Iron the bonding web in the centre of the calico square. Lay the square on a cork board. Cut the red ribbon into strips and lay these diagonally across the bonding web. Pin in position.

2 Weave strips of green ribbon diagonally through the red strips in the opposite direction. Press with an iron to bond and remove the pins. Stitch around the edge to secure the strips.

3 Trace the template from the back of the book. Cut three graduated fleur-de-lys shapes out of the felt. Place the smallest in the middle of the square and lay the larger pieces on top. Pin.

4 Stretch the panel in an embroidery hoop. Stitch around the felt with small hemming stitches, bringing the needle up close to the felt and down through the edge.

5 Cut the bullion into small pieces. Thread alternate types on to the needle, one at a time, and stitch down like beads in a random pattern all over the felt.

6 Couch two strands of gold metallic thread around the edge of the fleur-de-lys, leaving 5 cm/2 in ends on the right side. Couch the strands at the corners.

7 Use a large-eyed needle to pull the ends through to the reverse side. Trim and stitch securely. Trim the edge of the panel close to the machine stitching.

8 Lay the panel on top of the padded box insert and pin on all sides. Stitch two opposite edges together and pull up tightly. Repeat with the two other edges. Insert in the lid and screw in position.

CHERUB BOX

As the trend for paint effects gains momentum, unpainted fibreboard forms are becoming more readily available and can be found in many outlets. This small hinged box has a classic look, which is enhanced by gilding. It is given a baroque appearance by the addition of the cherub.

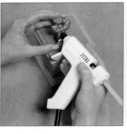

YOU WILL NEED

MATERIALS
cherub Christmas decoration
small wooden box with hinge
red oxide paint
water-based size
gold Dutch metal leaf
methylated spirit
amber shellac varnish
pink acrylic paint

EQUIPMENT
glue gun and glue sticks
paintbrushes
burnishing brush or soft cloth
steel wool
soft cloth
paint-mixing container

1 Use a glue gun to stick the cherub at an angle on the top of the box. Allow to dry for 10 minutes.

2 Prime the box with red oxide paint and allow to dry for several hours.

3 Paint on a thin, even coat of water-based size and leave for 20–30 minutes until it becomes clear and tacky.

4 Gild the surface with gold Dutch metal leaf, ensuring that the whole area is covered. Burnish with a brush or soft cloth to remove the excess leaf and bring up the lustre.

5 Dip some steel wool into methylated spirit and gently rub to reveal some of the base coat. Seal with a thin even coat of amber shellac and allow to dry for 30–60 minutes.

6 Mix some pink paint with water and paint over the surface. Rub off most of the paint with a cloth, leaving only a little paint in the details. Allow to dry for 30 minutes.

OAK LEAF BOX

This dressing table box uses a charming oak leaf motif for its decoration. The design is completed with hand-painted brushstrokes.

YOU WILL NEED

MATERIALS
round wooden box, with lid
emulsion (latex) paints: deep
blue-green, deep red and
dusky-pink
leaf stamp
clear satin varnish

EQUIPMENT
paintbrush
plates
foam rollers
square-tipped artist's brush
fine lining brush

1 Paint the box and lid in deep blue-green and allow to dry. Spread some deep red paint on a plate and run the roller through it until it is evenly coated. Ink the leaf stamp and stamp leaf motifs around the sides of the box.

2 Stamp two leaves in the centre of the box lid, side by side and facing in opposite directions. Use the square-tipped brush to paint a border around the top edge of the lid. Paint the sides of the lid in the same colour.

3 Using a fine lining brush and dusky-pink, paint veins on the leaves and a fine line around the inside edge of the red border.

4 When the paint is completely dry, seal the box with a coat of satin varnish.

VALENTINE BOXES

*Send your sweetheart
a special gift in one
of these lidded boxes.*

YOU WILL NEED

MATERIALS
*ovenproof bowl
vegetable fat or cooking oil
1 quantity salt dough
baking parchment
acrylic gesso or matt emulsion
(latex) paint
acrylic or craft paints
polyurethane satin varnish*

EQUIPMENT
*rolling pin
small, sharp knife
baking tray
biscuit cutter
paintbrushes*

1 Grease the upturned bowl. Roll out the dough on baking parchment to 1 cm/½ in thick. Mould it over the dish and cut away any excess. Smooth with a moistened finger.

2 Roll four balls of dough, moisten them slightly and press into the base of the bowl as "feet". Place the bowl on a tray and bake for nine hours at 120°C/250°F/ Gas ½.

3 Cut out a circle for the lid and a heart for the handle from the dough. Bake for about 45 minutes, then leave to cool. Attach the heart to the lid with wet dough. Bake for nine hours.

4 Allow all pieces to cool, then paint an undercoat on the bowl and lid. Paint on your own designs and colours and allow to dry. Seal with five coats of varnish inside and outside.

PAINTED SEWING BOX

This sewing box was inspired by one made by an Amish woman as a wedding gift. The legs are aptly made from old wooden cotton reels. Any oblong box with a hinged lid would be suitable.

YOU WILL NEED

MATERIALS
*4 wooden cotton reels
wooden box, with hinged lid
thin nails
wood glue
white emulsion (latex) paint
tracing paper
masking tape
artist's acrylic or stencil paints:
cobalt-blue, raw umber,
emerald-green, blue, deep and
light red, light blue, yellow-
ochre and white
clear water-based varnish*

EQUIPMENT
*hammer
paintbrushes
paint-mixing container
pencil
scissors
raised wooden batten (optional)*

1 Attach the cotton reels to the corners of the box with nails and some wood glue. Tint the white paint with a squeeze of cobalt-blue and raw umber.

2 Apply the emulsion (latex) paint to the outside of the box and the inside of the lid. Allow to dry. Trace the template from the back of the book. Cut out and transfer to the box, using masking tape to hold it in place.

3 The decoration on the box is very informal and painterly. Let your brush-strokes flow and embellish the decoration to suit yourself.

4 Select initials from the alphabet and paint them as solid shapes in blue. Allow them to dry, then outline the edges in dark red. Decorate the letters as shown.

5 Paint thick stripes with red. It is important to paint these stripes in a single brushstroke. It may be helpful to support your hand on a raised wooden batten.

6 Allow the stripes to dry, then outline the red with light blue lines, crossing over to form boxes in the corners. Tint the varnish with raw umber and sienna and then varnish the box.

HAND-PAINTED BOX

Decorate a wooden box with simple paint techniques that produce a wonderful effect reminiscent of inlaid wood patterns or marquetry, and turn it into a real treasure chest. This technique can apply both to old or new wooden furniture, picture frames, or even floors, provided that you strip down to bare wood and lighten with wood bleach, if necessary. The skill lies in developing your own pleasing pattern.

YOU WILL NEED

MATERIALS
bare wooden box, stripped, and bleached, if necessary
waterproof metallic or glossy paint
2 contrasting wood stains, such as brown mahogany and light teak
button polish or clear varnish
wax polish

EQUIPMENT
chalk
pen
small and fine paintbrushes
soft cloths

1 Trace the templates from the back of the book, enlarging to fit your box if necessary. Cover the backs of the templates with chalk, position them and trace around the outlines firmly with a pen.

2 Soak the paintbrushes, to rid them of loose bristles. Paint on the outlines in metallic or glossy paint and allow to dry. Fill in the areas between with the wood stains, flooding them up to the outlines. Do not overload the brush. Dry.

3 Coat lightly with button polish or wipe on varnish with a soft cloth. Then apply a few coats of wax polish to bring up the sheen and warmth of the wood.

SUN-GILDED BOX

*A gilded sun graces the lid of a plain wooden box
with a touch of celestial mystery. This luxurious
effect is easily achieved using Dutch gold leaf.
Delineate the gilding area with size to provide an
adhesive background, then apply the Dutch
gold as a transfer.*

YOU WILL NEED

MATERIALS	EQUIPMENT
wooden box	*medium and fine paintbrushes*
acrylic gesso	*sandpaper*
ultramarine acrylic paint	
gloss varnish	
Japanese gold size	
Dutch gold leaf transfer book	
silver leaf transfer book	

1 Paint the box, inside and
out, with three or more
coats of acrylic gesso, using a
medium brush (too many
coats may stop the lid from
closing properly, so be
careful). Allow to dry
thoroughly.

2 Give the box a coat of
ultramarine acrylic paint,
using a fine brush. When
dry, lightly sand to give a
distressed effect. Add a coat
of varnish.

3 Paint a freehand sun motif
on the lid, using the fine
brush and the gold size.
When the surface is just
tacky, place the gold leaf
transfer on top and rub
gently with a finger. Using
the same technique, paint
the side of the lid and loose,
freehand moons around the
sides of the box. Apply silver
leaf transfer and allow to dry.

FABRIC
FURNISHINGS

*Creating furnishings out of fabric is a beautiful method of decoration,
and it can be applied to a wide range of objects, including cushions,
curtains and linen. The wealth of threads available today means that
your furnishings can be bright and vivid or muted and subtle –
whatever mood you wish to evoke, there will be a thread and
fabric available for you.*

*The range of fabrics in varying colours, textures and strengths
is quite astounding, and you can choose the exact pieces
to suit your existing decor.*

MATERIALS AND EQUIPMENT

Most of the materials used for furnishing can be purchased from craft suppliers or department stores. The range of fabrics available is immense, so consider how the texture will affect your finished piece when making your fabric choice. Cotton and silk are easy to handle, and felt, plastic and leather produce interesting results. Some key materials and pieces of equipment to help you with your furnishing are given below.

Buttons and beads come in a range of shapes and sizes and a variety of materials, such as plastic, glass, wood and bone.

Carpenter's square is used for squaring fabrics, especially hems and seams.

Corner turner is a useful tool for making crisp creases and turning points.

Craft knife is used to cut paper and card templates and stencils.

Dressmaker's carbon is used to transfer designs to fabric.

Embroidery hoops A wooden hand embroidery hoop can also be used for machine embroidery if the inner ring is wrapped with strips of cotton to improve tautness.

Fabric glue can be used instead of fusible bonding web.

Fabric paints and pens are water-based non-toxic paints and pens that are fixed by ironing. Paints can be mixed and applied with brushes, while pens are easier and cleaner to use.

Fusible bonding web is used to bond appliqué fabrics to the ground fabric temporarily during stitching. Templates and motifs can be marked out with pen or pencil on the paper backing.

Machine embroidery threads are available in a myriad of colours and in different strengths. They are more lustrous than sewing threads. Metallic embroidery threads are also available.

Needles are available in many sizes. Use specialized needles with wide eyes when working with wool or embroidery threads.

Scissors Use dressmaker's scissors for cutting fabrics and embroidery scissors for cutting away threads and trimming.

Sewing machine A basic sewing machine with a normal stitching foot, zip foot, piping foot and darning foot is required for basic sewing. For machine embroidery, the machine should have a free arm and a detachable bed for ease of movement.

Staple gun Use a special heavyweight stapler to apply fabric to wood, when covering pelmets (valances) and screens, for example.

Stencil paper or card is available from artists' suppliers.

Stitch ripper Use one to quickly unpick stitches.

Tape measure is useful for measuring fabric and around curves.

Vanishing fabric markers are available in pink and purple and will fade with exposure to air or water.

BELOW *Working with fabrics and soft furnishings it's possible to make an impact using only simple craft skills. This is some of the basic equipment you will need.*

WORKING WITH DIFFERENT STITCHES

The basic skills of traditional sewing rely on a methodical approach. They are easy to learn and, with a bit of practice, will give a professional look to any piece of needlework. Careful pressing of the work at each stage will also help to ensure a good appearance.

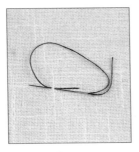

Backstitch

This is used in hand sewing to join together seams. It is also used in decorative embroidery to produce a slightly raised linear stitch for outlining areas of work.

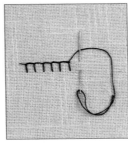

Blanket stitch

This can be used for finishing hems and when the stitches are worked closely together, for buttonholes. It is used decoratively for scalloped edging. Working from left to right, bring the needle down vertically and loop the thread under its tip before pulling it through.

Feather stitch

This is a looped stitch, traditionally used for smocking and decorating crazy patchwork. It can be worked in straight or curved lines. Bring the thread through the fabric and make slanting stitches, working alternately to the right and left of the line to be covered.

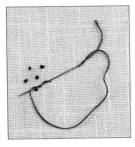

French knot

These are used sparingly as accents or worked more closely together to produce a texture. The stitch should be worked with the fabric in a frame, leaving both hands free. Bring the thread through and hold down. Twist the thread around the needle five times and tighten. Holding the thread taut, insert the needle back into the fabric with the other hand, at the point from which it emerged. Pull the needle through to form the knot.

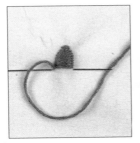

Satin stitch

This is used for filling in and outlining. Ensure the fabric is held tautly in a frame to prevent puckering. Carry the thread across the area to be filled, then return it back underneath the fabric as near as possible to the point from which the needle emerged.

Slip stitch

This is used to join together two folded edges and for flat hemming a turned-in edge. It should be nearly invisible. Pick up two threads of the single fabric and slip the needle through the fold for about 5 mm/¼ in. Draw the thread through to make a tiny stitch.

Tacking

This is a temporary stitch, used to hold seams together before sewing by machine. The stitches should be between 0.5–1 cm/¼–½ in long and evenly spaced. Use a contrasting thread to make the stitching easy to unpick.

ENGLISH LION CUSHION

Choose toning velvets in glowing "antique" colours for this sumptuous cushion, which will add a touch of historic grandeur to a room. The glittering metallic organza used for the lion gives him a subtle gilded look.

YOU WILL NEED

MATERIALS
tracing paper
tissue paper
tacking (basting) thread
cotton velvet fabrics:
32 x 43 cm/12½ x 17 in
deep red,
32 x 88 cm/12½ x 34½ in
orange
metallic organza,
32 x 43 cm/12½ x 17 in
metallic machine
embroidery thread
matching sewing thread
70 cm/28 in fringing
cushion pad,
28 x 55 cm/11 x 21½ in

EQUIPMENT
pencil
needle
embroidery hoop
sewing machine, with
darning foot
scissors
dressmaker's pins

1 Trace the template from the back of the book and transfer to tissue paper. Tack (baste) the tissue to the wrong side of the red velvet and the right side of the organza. Stretch in an embroidery hoop. Using the free embroidery mode and metallic thread, machine stitch the design. Remove the tissue and tacking (basting). On the right side, trim away the organza from the outer edge of the motif. Put the piece back in the hoop, right side up, and sew a narrow zigzag stitch to cover the edges.

2 Cut two strips of orange velvet 32 x 11 cm/12½ x 4¼ in. With right sides together, stitch these to either end of the panel. Cut two pieces of orange velvet, 32 x 48 cm/12½ x 19 in and 32 x 18 cm/12½ x 7 in for the back. Stitch a narrow double hem on the overlapping edges. Position the fringing along both short ends of the panel and pin in place. With right sides together, pin the backing pieces to the front, overlapping the hemmed edges. Stitch, trim, turn to the right side and insert the pad.

SILK CUSHION COVER

A spectacular flower head makes a really bold statement on this cushion cover. It would look wonderful in a light, bright, modern design scheme. The drama of the overall conception is balanced by the delicacy of the hand-painted effect.

YOU WILL NEED

MATERIALS
*double-sided tape
white silk-satin, 2½ times the width of the cushion pad, plus 1.5 cm /⅝ in seam allowance
silk paints: yellow, red, blue, turquoise and ultramarine
matching silk thread*

EQUIPMENT
*fine-art stretchers or large frame scissors
vanishing fabric marker or tailor's chalk
paint-mixing container
large flat-bristled, medium and fine paintbrushes
sewing machine
dressmaker's pins
needle
iron*

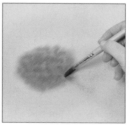

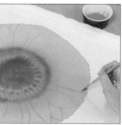

1 Fix double-sided tape all around the stretchers or frame. Fold the silk-satin into three panels, two the width of the pad and one half the width (to form the flap). Mark the panels with marker or chalk. Stretch the silk on the frame so that the front (the middle panel) is centred on the frame. Brush yellow paint from the centre outwards, using the flat brush.

2 Straight away, before the paint dries, add red paint to the yellow to make orange and redefine the centre part of the circle. Add blue to make a green and make a smaller circle in the centre of the orange. Add dots in the centre with more blue. Allow to dry.

3 Define the petals with red. Fill in the background with shades of blue. Turn under, and stitch a double hem on each short edge. Fold the silk back into its original panels with right sides facing, so that the flap covers half the front. Fold the back over both and pin and stitch the side seams. Turn the cover right sides out, insert the pad and slip stitch the gap.

STENCILLED TABLECLOTH

Two stencils are arranged here to decorate a square tablecloth; the same motifs could be used in many different combinations and scales. Use two or three shades with each stencil shape to achieve a rounded, three-dimensional look on the roses and branches.

YOU WILL NEED

MATERIALS	EQUIPMENT
tracing paper	*pencil*
stencil card	*craft knife*
heavy white cotton fabric,	*cutting mat*
76 x 76 cm / 30 x 30 in	*iron*
stencil paints: dark and pale	*spray adhesive*
pink, yellow, dark and light	*3 stencil brushes*
green and warm brown	*vanishing fabric marker*
white sewing thread	*long ruler*
	set square
	needle

1 Trace the rose template from the back of the book, enlarging to 15 cm/6 in across. Enlarge the branch template so it is 30 cm/12 in long. Transfer both to stencil card and cut out the stencils.

2 Fold the fabric in half each way to find the centre. Press lightly along the creases. Spray the back of the rose stencil lightly with adhesive and place it in the middle of the cloth. Paint dark pink in the corner petals and carefully around the outer edge of the inner petals.

3 Fill in the rest of the petals with pale pink and colour the centre dots yellow. Keep the brush upright and use a small circling motion to transfer the paint. Be careful not to overload the bristles. Peel off the stencil and allow the paint to dry.

4 Work a branch motif on each side of the rose, using the crease as a placement guide, to form a cross. Spray the back of the card with adhesive, as before. Stencil yellow paint in the centre of each leaf.

5 Blend dark and light green paints and finish painting the leaves.

6 Work a small amount of brown around the base of the leaves and the outside edge of the branches. Stencil a rose at the end of each branch.

7 With a fabric marker, and using the ruler and set square to get a perfectly accurate square, draw a line about 15 cm/6 in from each edge, so that it is on the same level as the outer edge of the roses. Stencil a rose in each corner and then work a branch between the roses.

8 When the paint is dry, fix it according to the manufacturer's instructions. Turn under, press and stitch a narrow double hem along the outside edge.

FRUITY APPLIQUE CUSHION

A bright, graphic cushion which would be ideal for a kitchen, a sunny garden bench or conservatory.

YOU WILL NEED

MATERIALS
*orange cotton fabric,
60 x 15 cm/24 x 6 in
yellow cotton fabric,
45 x 15 cm/18 x 6 in
green cotton fabric,
30 x 15 cm/12 x 6 in
matching sewing thread
tracing paper
fusible bonding web
craft felt: orange, yellow and
4 shades of green
blue and white cotton,
60 x 90 cm/24 x 36 in
5 self-cover buttons
50 cm/20 in cushion pad*

EQUIPMENT
*dressmaker's scissors
sewing machine
iron and pressing cloth
pencil
dressmaker's pins
needle*

1 Cut the cotton fabric into 15 cm/6 in squares: four orange, three yellow and two green. Machine stitch together in three rows of three, with a 1 cm/½ in seam allowance. Press the seams open. Join the three strips into a square, carefully matching the seams, and press the long seams open.

2 Trace the template from the back of the book, enlarging it as necessary. Transfer the leaf and fruit to the backing paper of the bonding web. Cut the shapes out roughly and iron on to the different coloured felts, then cut out accurately along the outlines.

3 Peel off the backing paper and place the shapes on the coloured squares, arranging the leaves so that they lie under the orange and yellow circles. Iron in place following the manufacturer's instructions.

4 Trace the shapes for the second layer of appliqué shapes – the orange slices, leaf veins and the star-shaped trim for the whole oranges – on to the bonding web. Cut out from felt as before and press in place.

7 Fold the two back panels to the wrong side, leaving a 6 cm/2½ in check border at the front of the cushion cover. Pin and stitch the seams, leaving a 1 cm/½ in seam allowance. Turn to the right side and press. Sew the buttons in place, insert the pad and do up the buttons.

5 From the check fabric, cut two 53 x 45 cm/21 x 18 in rectangles and two strips of 8 x 40 cm/3¼ x 16 in. Sew the two strips along opposite sides of the appliqué square. Turn under and stitch a double hem along one long side of each large rectangle. Make five evenly spaced buttonholes along one hemmed edge, then, with right sides facing, sew the unfinished long edges to the other two sides of the square.

6 Following the button manufacturer's instructions, cover each of the five buttons in a different coloured felt.

MUSLIN (CHEESECLOTH) CURTAIN

Felt stars are caught in the deep hem of this unusual, sheer curtain. When machining them in, match the sewing thread to each of the colours of the felt.

YOU WILL NEED

MATERIALS
tracing paper
thin card or paper
felt squares: purple, light, medium and dark blue, light and dark pink
white muslin (cheesecloth), to fit window, plus 36 cm / 14 in
matching machine embroidery threads
curtain tape

EQUIPMENT
pencil
scissors
tailor's chalk
iron
dressmaker's pins
tacking (basting) thread
needle
sewing machine

1 Trace the template from the back of the book, enlarging if necessary, transfer to thin card or paper and cut out. Using tailor's chalk, draw two stars on each felt colour and cut out.

2 Make a 25 cm/10 in hem in the muslin (cheesecloth) and press along the fold. Open it out and arrange the felt stars above the fold line and within the depth of the hem.

3 Carefully pin the hem back over the stars, turning under 1 cm/½ in along the raw edge. Pin the stars in position and tack (baste) around the edges 5 mm/¼ in outside the felt.

4 Machine stitch around each star using matching thread. Sew the ends under the muslin (cheesecloth) and trim. Stitch the hem and add curtain tape at the top of the curtain.

ASTROLOGICAL CUSHION

This cover achieves its effect with a combination of metallic fabric and embroidery. The fabric creates a rich impression, but machine embroidery makes the cover quite straightforward to achieve. This cushion is bound to induce a feeling of tranquillity when you settle down for a nap.

YOU WILL NEED

MATERIALS	EQUIPMENT
brown velvet	tape measure
cushion pad	dressmaker's scissors
matching thread	sewing machine, with darning
matching zip	foot
gold metallic organza	vanishing fabric marker
matching machine embroidery	embroidery hoop
thread	needle
tracing paper	
press (snap) fasteners	

1 For the front, cut one piece of velvet to the size of the cushion pad plus 2 cm/ ¾ in all round. For the back, cut two pieces of velvet each to half the width of the front piece, plus a 2 cm/¾ in allowance on both centre back edges.

2 Join the two pieces and insert a zip. Lay the front and back right sides together and stitch all round the outside. Cut one front and two back pieces of organza as before. Turn under and stitch a double hem of 1 cm/½ in on each centre edge of the back pieces. Trace the template from the back of the book, enlarging if necessary. Put the front organza piece over the design and trace it on the fabric with a fabric marker.

3 Select the darning or free embroidery mode on the sewing machine and place the organza in a hoop. Stitch around the shapes with gold embroidery thread.

4 With right sides facing, stitch the organza pieces together. Stitch on the press (snap) fasteners. Insert the cushion pad in the velvet and insert the cushion in the organza.

CAFE-STYLE CURTAIN

An attractive, eye-catching curtain that hangs over the lower half of a window, with a scalloped heading and simple fabric loops.

YOU WILL NEED

MATERIALS
*curtain pole
fabric for curtain
facing fabric
matching machine thread
card*

EQUIPMENT
*tape measure
dressmaker's scissors
sewing machine
dressmaker's pins
craft knife
cutting mat
iron
fabric marker
needle*

1 Measure the length of the pole. Cut one width of fabric to this length plus an 8 cm/3¼ in hem allowance, by the length of the drop from the pole to the window sill, plus a 20 cm/8 in hem allowance and 10 cm/4 in extra for the fabric loops. Join widths together if necessary. Cut facing fabric to the same width by 40 cm/16 in long. On the facing, press and turn under a hem of 5 mm/¼ in. Machine stitch. Pin the curtain and the facing, right sides facing.

2 Cut out a card scallop template to your required size. Divide the curtain width by the width of the scallop and the strips in between – these should be 4–7 cm/1½–2¾ in – to calculate the number of scallops needed. The curtain should have a strip at each end. Place the top of the scallop template at the top of the curtain and mark around it with a fabric marker. Work across the curtain, placing the scallops a strip-width apart.

3 Machine stitch the facing to the curtain along the marked line. Trim to 1 cm/½ in from the stitching and clip the corners and into the curves.

4 Turn the work right sides out. Top stitch across the top 5 mm/¼ in from the edge.

5 Turn and press a double hem of 2 cm/¾ in along each side of the curtain. Turn and press a double hem of 5 cm/2 in at the bottom of the curtain. Mitre the corners and machine or slip stitch the hem in place. Turn and press under a single hem of 4 cm/1½ in on both sides of the facing. Slip stitch the facing and all the hems in place.

6 To make fabric loops, turn the strip to the wrong side by 5 cm/2 in and machine stitch to the facing.

SEA PILLOWCASE

*Rainbow yarn, in which
a variety of beautifully
toning shades are
combined in one length,
is couched with
embroidery thread to
create lovely sea-toned
shell shapes on this
special pillowcase.*

YOU WILL NEED

MATERIALS
*tracing paper
pillowcase, with flanges and
decorative embroidery line
rainbow yarn
stranded embroidery threads:
pale blue , blue-green and dark
blue
iron-on interfacing*

EQUIPMENT
*dressmaker's pins
transfer pen
small, fine embroidery and
tapestry or large-eyed needle
iron*

1 Trace the template from
the back of the book,
enlarging if necessary. Mark
the positions of the shell
motifs on the pillowcase
with pins. Transfer to the
pillowcase.

2 Cut the rainbow yarn into
separate colours. Use a single
strand of pale blue to couch
the blue threads, and the
same of blue-green for the
green-blue shades. Couch a
single pale blue thread
between the bands of colour.

3 Using a large-eyed or
tapestry needle, pull the ends
through to the wrong side.
Iron interfacing on to
secure.

4 Weave a thread of dark
blue thread through the
decorative stitching.

SCENTED CUSHION

A regal little cushion fit for a Leo. When stuffing the cushion, you can either scent the wadding (batting) with a few drops of essential oil, or pack a small amount of pot-pourri in among the filling.

YOU WILL NEED

MATERIALS
*tracing paper
cream cotton fabric,
23 x 23 cm/9 x 9 in
tear-off interfacing,
23 x 23 cm/9 x 9 in
stranded embroidery
cotton: black and 5 graduated
shades of yellow and gold
dark blue velvet,
34 x 17 cm/13 x 6½ in
matching sewing thread
gold cord, 38 cm/15 in
polyester toy wadding (batting)
essential oil or pot-pourri
4 gold tassels*

EQUIPMENT
*pencil
transfer pen
needle
embroidery hoop
iron
scissors*

1 Trace the template from the back of the book, enlarge it, and transfer to the cotton fabric. Tack (baste) the tear-off interfacing to the back and mount in a hoop.

2 Using two strands of embroidery thread, work the two circles in split stitch in dark gold, then outline the lion and zodiac symbols in black using straight and split stitch. Fill in the background with long and short stitch, blending the colours from light to dark gold.

3 Remove the hoop and press the embroidery lightly on the wrong side. Cut out, leaving a 5 mm/¼ in seam allowance. Clip the curves and tack (baste) the allowance to the back.

4 Cut the velvet into two 17 cm/6½ in squares. Tack (baste) and stitch the motif to the centre front of one square. Slip stitch the gold cord around the circle. Make a small slit in the velvet and push the two ends to the wrong side. Sew over the slit and unpick the tacking (basting) threads.

5 With right sides together, join three sides. Clip the corners and turn. Fill with scented polyester wadding (batting). Slip stitch the opening and sew a tassel to each corner.

SILK-PAINTED CURTAIN

*This sheer curtain is an unusual alternative to nets,
allowing in the light, yet masking the window.
Gutta forms a strong outline that stops the
paints bleeding into each other.*

YOU WILL NEED

MATERIALS

*tracing paper
lining paper
clear plastic sheeting
white cotton muslin
(cheesecloth) fabric
masking tape
gutta
iron-fixed silk paints: deep
blue, bright green and yellow
strong sewing thread
1 cm/½ in cotton hemming
tape
curtain-weighting cord*

EQUIPMENT

*scissors
pencil
pipette with a fine nib
fine paintbrushes
paint-mixing containers
iron and pressing cloth
spray starch
sewing machine
needle*

1 Trace the templates from
the back of the book,
enlarging if necessary. Cut
the lining paper, plastic
sheeting and the fabric to fit
your window. Arrange the
templates on the lining paper
and draw around them. Then
draw seaweed freehand, to
pull the design together. Put
the plastic on top and the
fabric on top of that. Secure
with masking tape.

2 Apply the gutta to the
muslin (cheesecloth), using
the pipette and following the
outlines on the lining paper.
Press firmly. It is important
for the gutta line to be solid,
to prevent the paint from
bleeding. Check for any gaps
or thin lines.

3 When the gutta is dry,
paint in the coloured areas
with the silk paints. Leave to
dry thoroughly.

4 Iron the curtain, to fix the
paints, according to the
manufacturer's instructions.
Wash the curtain and apply
spray starch when it is dry.

5 Apply the hemming tape
to neaten the edges. Insert
the weighting cord in the
bottom hem. Make a casing
for the heading by turning
over the edge and applying
hemming tape to the seam.

NURSERY CUSHION

This is a delightful cushion that would lend a touch of jollity to any nursery and would also make a lovely accessory for a bedroom chair.

YOU WILL NEED

MATERIALS
tracing paper
dressmaker's carbon paper
white sprigged cotton fabric,
42 x 42 cm / 16½ x 16½ in
3 skeins dark red stranded
embroidery thread
4 strips darker patterned
cotton fabric,
1 m x 14 cm / 1 yd x 5½ in
matching and contrasting
sewing threads
2 rectangles plain cotton,
30 x 42 cm / 12 x 16½ in
dark red velvet ribbon,
120 cm / 48 in cushion pad,
40 x 40 cm / 16 x 16 in

EQUIPMENT
pencil
embroidery hoop
needle
sewing machine
dressmaker's pins

1 Trace the template from the back of the book and enlarge to the desired size. Transfer to the sprigged cotton fabric, using dressmaker's carbon paper. Stretch the fabric in a hoop and embroider the outline in chain stitch. To make the frill, join the darker fabric strips together and hem one long edge.

2 Run a gathering thread along the edge opposite the hem. With right sides together, pin the gathers to the embroidered cushion front, matching the four joins to the four corners. Draw up the gathering thread until the frill fits the cushion, pin and stitch.

3 For the backing, stitch a double hem along one long side of each rectangle of plain fabric. With right sides together, place one rectangle at each end of the embroidered front, so that the hemmed edges lie to the centre. Pin and stitch around the outer edge, leaving a small seam allowance.

4 Turn the cushion the right way out. Make four bows from the velvet ribbon. Sew to the corners of the cushion and insert the pad.

BAROQUE VELVET CUSHION

Use richly coloured velvets and gold braid to create a gorgeous baroque cushion.

YOU WILL NEED

MATERIALS
2 coloured paper cupid motifs
white cotton fabric,
30 x 40 cm/12 x 16 in
image transfer fluid
fabric glue
blue velvet,
42 x 62 cm/16½ x 25 in
metallic machine embroidery
threads: gold and red
red velvet scraps
1 cm/½ in wide gold braid,
40 cm/16 in
2 pearl-drop beads
gold cord, 50 cm/20 in
matching sewing threads
2 squares matching taffeta,
42 x 42 cm/16½ x 16½ in
3 cm/1¼ in wide wire-edged
red ribbon, 2 m/2 yd
cushion pad
40 x 60 cm/16 x 24 in

EQUIPMENT
dressmaker's scissors
sewing machine
needle

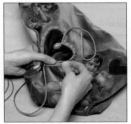

1 Follow the manufacturer's instructions to transfer the cupid motifs to the cotton fabric with image transfer fluid. Cut out each cupid and glue in place on the velvet. Machine stitch the edges with zigzag stitch using gold thread. Cut one large and two small hearts from the red velvet. Stitch as before, using fine red metallic thread.

2 Stitch gold braid around the larger heart. Sew a pearl-drop bead to the top and bottom of the heart and trim with gold cord, looping it around the beads. Stitch the cord in place.

3 Make the backing for the cushion with the two squares of taffeta, as described in the Nursery Cushion project. Clip the corners and turn the work the right way out. Cut the wire-edged ribbon into four equal lengths and tie them into bows. Trim the ends to V-shapes and stitch one to each corner. Insert the cushion pad.

PEG BAG

This peg bag is made from practical unbleached calico. The sunflowers are worked in dry stencil fabric paint. Once they are fixed, the stencils will be hand-washable.

YOU WILL NEED

MATERIALS

tracing paper
stencil card
unbleached calico,
50 x 75 cm / 20 x 30 in
child's wooden coat hanger,
30 cm / 12 in
dry stencil fabric paints:
yellow and brown
matching machine
embroidery thread
yellow ribbon, 1 m / 1 yd

EQUIPMENT

soft and hard pencils
craft knife
cutting mat
dressmaker's scissors
dressmaker's pins
vanishing fabric marker
2 stencil brushes
iron
sewing machine
needle

1 Trace the template from the back of the book, enlarging it if necessary to the desired size necessary. Transfer the outline to stencil card and cut out. From the unbleached calico, cut two squares, each 36 cm / 14 in in size.

2 Pin the squares together, place the hanger along one edge and draw round it with the marker. Cut this curve. Stencil a sunflower in each corner of one piece of fabric. Allow the paint to dry and fix it, according to the manufacturer's instructions.

3 Cut a 10 x 25 cm / 4 x 10 in piece of calico facing for the front opening. Tack (baste) the facing on to the centre top of the stencilled fabric. Sew two 20 cm / 8 in lines of straight stitch, 5 mm / ¼ in away from both sides of the centre. Cut in between these lines, and turn the facing to the wrong side. Press and top stitch around the opening.

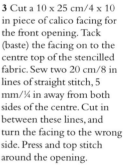

4 With right sides together, stitch the back to the front. Turn right sides out, fit the coat hanger in place and finish off with a yellow bow.

QUILTED CUSHION

The classic Tudor rose
motif is picked out in
quilting lines on this
vibrant silk cushion; the
traditional rosy red
colour makes a perfect
complement for this
regal motif.

YOU WILL NEED

MATERIALS
tracing paper
red silk taffeta,
100 x 90 cm/40 x 36 in
calico,
100 x 90 cm/40 x 36 in
wadding (batting),
50 x 50 cm/20 x 20 in
tacking (basting) thread
red sewing thread
piping cord, 1.5 m/1½ yd
polyester stuffing (batting)

EQUIPMENT
fine black felt-tipped pen
tape measure
dressmaking scissors
quilter's pencil
needle
dressmaker's pins
sewing machine
iron

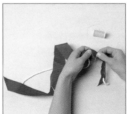

1 Trace the template from
the back of the book,
enlarging it as necessary.
Outline the rose in black
pen. Cut a 50 cm/20 in
square of silk. Lay the silk on
top and trace the rose

directly on to the fabric with
a quilter's pencil. Cut a 50
cm/20 in square of calico.
Layer the wadding (batting)
between the calico and the
silk. Tack (baste) the layers
together with lines of stitches
radiating from the centre.

2 Quilt along the lines of the
design outline in red thread,
working from the centre out.
Once complete, draw a five-
sided shape around the
design and trim the cushion
along the lines.

3 Cut and join 5 cm/2 in
bias strips from red silk. Press
the seams open and trim.
Fold the strip over the
piping cord and tack (baste)
along it. Next, pin and tack
(baste) the piping around the

cushion edge, with raw
edges together. Machine
stitch along one side, close to
the piping. Lay a square of
silk and then calico on the
right side of the cushion.

4 Pin, tack (baste) and stitch
round the edges, leaving a
small gap. Trim the seams
and corners and turn
through. Fill with stuffing
(batting) and slip stitch the
gap closed.

PAINTED TABLECLOTH

Choose a fine white or cream linen, lawn or cambric for this cloth. The birds are painted with fabric paints and fixed by ironing; the cutwork is finished with a zigzag stitch in a contrasting colour.

YOU WILL NEED

MATERIALS

tracing paper
graph paper
stencil card
cotton or linen fabric, to fit table
water-based fabric paints
card
contrasting thread

EQUIPMENT

pencil
magic marker
iron
paintbrush
fabric marker
sewing machine
small, sharp scissors

1 Trace the templates from the back of the book, enlarging on graph to size. Redraw it with a magic marker on stencil card. Wash, dry and press the fabric.

2 Mark the position of the birds, spacing them evenly around the edge of the cloth. Position the template under the fabric and smooth out the fabric. Trace the design using fabric paint.

3 Fix the paint by ironing on the wrong side of the fabric, following the manufacturer's instructions. Draw around the scallop template along the edge of the cloth with a fabric marker.

4 With contrasting thread, stitch along the marked line and then machine stitch a close zigzag around the scallops. Trim the excess fabric down to the stitched edge using small scissors.

NEEDLEPOINT CUSHION

This cushion would be perfect for an easy chair in the kitchen. The cushion is worked in simple stitches, but they produce a really stylish effect.

YOU WILL NEED

MATERIALS
12-count, single-thread canvas, 25 cm / 10 in square
masking tape
tracing paper
2 skeins each 3-strand yarn: dark brown, 2 shades of mid-blue and light cream
1 skein each 3-strand yarn: light brown, light and dark yellow and warm light brown velvet polyester wadding (batting), 19 cm / 7½ in square
matching sewing thread

EQUIPMENT
pencil
scissors
felt-tipped pens
ruler
tapestry needle
dressmaker's pins
needle
drawing pins

1 Bind the edges of the canvas with masking tape. Trace the template from the back of the book, enlarging as required. Place the canvas over the tracing. Trace the main outline on the centre of the canvas, then fill in the detailed lines.

2 All the stitches are sewn with two strands of yarn. Work the main outline in dark brown tent stitch, and then fill in the petals with tent stitch and the flower centre with upright cross stitch. Rule a 16.5 cm/ 6½ in square around the flower and fill in the background with cushion stitch. Work with two different strands of blue together, and alternate blue and cream squares.

3 Block the canvas by spraying it lightly with water. Stretch and pin it squarely. When dry, trim the canvas to leave 1 cm/½ in all around the edge. Pin velvet to the backing, with right sides together. Stitch around three sides and turn right sides out. Insert the wadding (batting) and slip stitch the gap closed.

CUSHION WITH SEASHELLS

With this lovely cushion cover, the fluid curves of the seashells contrast strikingly with the regularity of the checks.

YOU WILL NEED

MATERIALS
tracing paper
fusible bonding web,
20 x 20 cm / 8 x 8 in
3 shades beige cotton scraps
light-tone cotton gingham,
25 x 25 cm / 10 x 10 in
embroidery threads
medium-tone cotton homespun
check,
25 x 35 cm / 10 x 14 in
matching sewing thread
unbleached calico,
60 x 100 cm / 24 x 40 in
dark-tone cotton homespun
check, 20 x 20 cm / 8 x 8 in
24 buttons
cushion pad

EQUIPMENT
pencil
dressmaker's scissors
sharp pencil
iron and pressing cloth
needle
dressmaker's pins
sewing machine

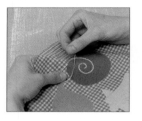

1 Trace the template from the back of the book. Place the bonding web on top and trace the motifs on to the fabric. Cut them out. Iron each shell on to a different scrap of plain cotton fabric. Cut out round each outline.

2 Using a sharp pencil, mark the curves and spirals on the right side of the shells. Peel off the backing paper and arrange the three shapes on the gingham square. Fuse by pressing with a cool iron and a pressing cloth.

3 Using three strands of embroidery thread and, working with small, regular stitches, embroider a line of chain stitches around the shell shapes, to cover the raw edges and pick out the marked details

4 Cut two strips of medium-tone cotton measuring 7 x 25 cm / 3 x 10 in. With right sides facing and leaving a seam allowance of 1 cm / ½ in, sew them to opposite sides of the gingham square. Press the seams open. Cut two strips, each 7 x 38 cm / 3 x 15 in. Pin and then sew them to the remaining two sides. Press the seams open.

5 Cut four strips of calico 10 x 38 cm / 4 x 15 in and four squares of dark-tone cotton 10 cm / 4 in. Stitch two strips to opposite sides of the main square, leaving a 1 cm / ½ in seam allowance and press the seams open. Sew a square to each end of the other strips and press the seams open. With right sides facing, sew in place and press the seams open.

6 Cut two rectangles of unbleached calico to make the back of the cushion, each 30 x 45 cm / 12 x 18 in. Hem one long side of each. With right sides facing, pin one rectangle to two opposite sides of the cushion front. Sew around the four edges, leaving a 1 cm / ½ in seam allowance. Clip the corners and turn the cover right side out.

7 Sew the buttons securely along the calico strips at 5 cm / 2 in intervals, using embroidery thread.

SHELF EDGING

Quick and simple, this pretty scalloped edging makes a feature of what would otherwise be a dull storage unit.

YOU WILL NEED

MATERIALS

tracing paper
stencil card
fabric, to fit shelf length plus a 2 cm /¾ in allowance by 13 cm 5½ in, plus the shelf depth plus a 2 cm /¾ in allowance
heavy-weight fusible interfacing, size of fabric
matching thread
bias binding

EQUIPMENT

pencil
craft knife
cutting mat
iron
dressmaker's pins
sewing machine
fabric marker

1 Trace the template from the back of the book, enlarging if necessary. Transfer to stencil card and cut out. Iron the interfacing to the wrong side of the fabric. On the top edge, press, pin and stitch a 1 cm/½ in double hem.

2 Lay the fabric strip on the table. Mark around the template with a fabric marker all along the length. Cut away the excess fabric.

3 Machine stitch the bias binding to the right side of the scalloped edge. Fold the bias binding over the fabric edge and slip stitch it to the wrong side.

4 Neaten the edging with a hem and pin it along the back edge of the shelf. Fold the fabric over the shelf edge and pin it at either side.

PAINTED SILK HANGING

Reminiscent of the stained-glass rose windows that are a feature of medieval churches and cathedrals, this design is created by making outlines of gutta and painting in between them. Bought silk scarves are useful here, because the edges are ready-rolled. Any kind of frame can be used for stretching, as long as it is large and strong enough to hold the silk stretched and flat.

YOU WILL NEED

MATERIALS
silk square
gutta
silk paints in a variety of colours

EQUIPMENT
frame
dressmaker's pins
vanishing fabric marker
pipette
fine-pointed watercolour paintbrush
iron

1 Wash the silk to remove all impurities and finish the edges if necessary. Stretch and pin the silk on to the frame on all sides.

2 Draw out your chosen design on the silk, using a fabric marker.

3 Apply the gutta, using a pipette. Make sure you press firmly and squeeze at the same time. It is important for the gutta line to be solid, to prevent the paint from bleeding. Check for any gaps and leave the gutta to dry.

4 After the gutta has dried, apply the silk paints. Allow to dry. Remove the silk from the frame and iron it to fix for a few minutes.

STELLAR TABLECLOTH

The tablecloth used here has a scalloped edging which makes for very even stamping – just count the scallops and then decide to stamp on, say, every third one.

YOU WILL NEED

MATERIALS
tablecloth and napkins
scrap of fabric
navy blue fabric stamping ink

EQUIPMENT
large and small star rubber stamps

1 Plan the position of your motifs. Coat the smaller stamp with fabric ink and make a test print on to a scrap of fabric first to ensure the stamp is not overloaded.

2 Make the first print by positioning a small star in one corner.

3 Stamp a large star on either side of it and continue along the edges, alternating the size of stars.

4 Stamp one widely spaced square of small stars about 10 cm/4 in in from the first row, and another square of large stars 10 cm/4 in closer to the centre. Aim for an all-over pattern with a border.

GARDEN APRON

For this project you may need access to a colour photocopier. A collection of prints of old botanical paintings would make a beautiful apron for a horticulturally minded friend.

YOU WILL NEED

MATERIALS
selection of colour images of leaves
cotton apron
masking tape (optional)
image transfer gel

EQUIPMENT
scissors
paintbrush
soft cloth

1 Make a selection of images and photocopy them in colour if you want to create a repeat pattern.

2 Cut around each leaf shape until you have enough to cover the apron.

3 Plan your design by positioning the leaves on the apron, face down. Secure with masking tape if required. Paint a thick layer of transfer gel on to the first motif.

4 Replace the image face down on the apron and rub with a soft cloth. Repeat with all the images and leave to transfer overnight. Soak the cloth with clean water and rub away the paper.

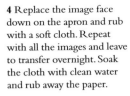

PATCHWORK THROW

This patchwork throw is an ideal way to use up odd remnants of furnishing fabrics. Your local upholsterer may sell off old sample books, which are a good source of different rose prints and contrasting weaves and textures.

YOU WILL NEED

MATERIALS
selection of rose-printed and plain fabrics
matching sewing thread
dusky red heavyweight Jacquard-weave fabric, 1.4 m/1 yd 16 in square
25 small buttons
woven furnishing braid, 4.75 m/5 yd 29 in

EQUIPMENT
iron
dressmaker's scissors
rotary cutter
quilter's square rule
cutting mat
sewing machine
dressmaker's pins and tacking (basting) thread, or safety pins
needle

1 Press the fabrics and cut out 18 plain and 18 patterned squares, each 20 cm/8 in square. For accuracy, use a rotary cutter and quilter's square for this.

2 Lay the pieces on the floor, to form a checkerboard of alternate plain and printed squares. Take time to find a pleasing pattern and balance of colours.

3 Sew rows of three squares together, leaving seam allowances of 1 cm/½ in. Press the seams open.

4 Sew three rows together, with the same seam allowances, matching the joins to assemble four blocks of three by three squares. Join the four blocks, to form a large square.

5 Square up the edges of the backing fabric. Fringe the edges by pulling away threads from each side.

6 Place the patchwork square in the centre of the backing fabric. Pin and tack (baste) or safety pin it securely in place.

7 Fix the patchwork in place by firmly sewing a button at each intersection point. Make sure that you sew right through all the layers of fabric.

8 Slip stitch the braid on to the backing to attach and conceal the raw edges. Mitre the corners as you sew.

Sprigged Calico Curtains

Natural calico has a lovely creamy colour, especially when the sun shines through. The stamped floral sprig used here lifts the humble fabric into another dimension.

You Will Need

MATERIALS
calico fabric
fabric stamping inks:
green and dark blue
paper
card
scrap of fabric

EQUIPMENT
linocut stamp
craft knife
cutting mat
ruler
pencil

1 Lay the fabric out on a flat surface. Make several prints of the stamp on scrap paper and cut them out. Plan the design on the fabric.

2 Decide on the distance you want between sprigs and cut out a square of card to act as a measuring guide. Use it diagonally, marking with a pencil at each corner all over the fabric.

3 Put green ink on the edges of the linocut and fill the centre with dark blue. Make an initial print on a scrap of fabric to determine the density of the image.

4 Stamp the floral sprig on to the calico. You need to apply gentle pressure to the back of the stamp and allow a couple of seconds for the ink to transfer.

CHILD'S BLANKET

Small children will love to snuggle up under this cosy blanket.

YOU WILL NEED

MATERIALS
blanket fabric
contrasting tapestry wool
assorted scraps of coloured woollen or blanket fabric
large buttons

EQUIPMENT
dressmaker's scissors
crewel needle
saucer

 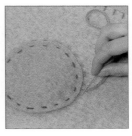 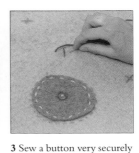

1 Cut the blanket to the size required, turn under a small hem and blanket stitch the edge with tapestry wool.

2 Draw around a saucer on to the scraps of fabric and cut out circles. Hand appliqué to the blanket in running stitch.

3 Sew a button very securely to the centre of each circle. Work large cross stitches in a contrasting colour to fill the background fabric.
Safety Note: Not for use with very young children, who may be tempted to chew on the buttons.

CREATIVE STATIONERY AND GIFT WRAPS

Working with paper is a truly satisfying and creative craft, and the bonus is that it can also be good for the environment, if you recycle old and used papers in your projects. There is such a wealth of colours, textures and sizes available in paper that the scope for producing wonderful decorations and gifts really is endless.

The projects in this book should inspire you to experiment with paper whatever your tastes and ability. The great thing about using paper to create stationery and gift wrap is that you can provide friends and family with personalized presents that suit them – your ideas are bound to make a refreshing change from the mass-produced equivalents.

MATERIALS AND EQUIPMENT

Using just a little imagination, it's possible to make your own stationery and gift wrapping with real style and flair. But, before you embark on the projects here, make a point of exploring some possible paper sources. Paper comes in many different weights, textures, patterns and colours – perhaps more so now than ever before. Try searching in art and hobby shops, printers, office stationers and specialist suppliers.

In this section, more than 20 projects show you how to embellish the paper you buy with techniques such as stamping, embossing, printing and collage. A craft knife and a cutting mat or a pair of paper scissors are vital when working with paper, and so too is masking tape as it won't tear the paper. Paper glue or spray adhesive are also useful to have at hand. On the page opposite you will find a basic kit that will show you what you need to use to tackle the projects in this book.

Painting and colouring your paper projects presents no problem, and there is a wide range of crayons, pens, paints and varnishes available that are suitable for paper. Just check the manufacturer's instructions before you apply the material to paper. You can always do a test run on a scrap of paper first, just to make sure, rather than spoil your design.

Working with different papers
Tissue and crepe paper are cheap papers sold at stationer's and craft suppliers. Tissue paper needs to be layered to build up intense colour. Crêpe paper is thicker and crinkly and its only drawback is that adhesive tape doesn't stick to it very well.

LEFT AND ABOVE *A selection of papers and decorative materials. Today there is a truly staggering range of paper types, weights and colours.*

Hand-printed paper All you need is plain paper and a spark of inspiration – and you may never buy gift wrap again. Potato cuts, rubber stamps, stencils, rollers or brushstrokes will all produce unique patterned papers. Use lightweight paper or cheap brown wrapping paper for the best results.
Corrugated card gives projects a unique texture and depth, and it is also very cheap to buy.
Natural papers are available now as so many sorts of handmade paper are being imported from the East; the selection really is enormous. It is possible to buy paper made from banana skins or recycled Bombay newsprint inlaid with rose petals. The colours are often hotter and spicier than home-produced papers, so it's well worth looking for a specialist paper outlet that carries a range of natural papers.

MATERIALS AND EQUIPMENT

Accessories and equipment
Creative stationery and gift wrap
involves more than a roll of
sticky tape and some patterned
paper. Here is a selection of
craft accessories you may need
to produce the best results.
Some you will find in an office
supply shop, others in an art
materials store.

Adhesive (cellophane) tape
Clear adhesive tape is best used with
materials such as ribbons, which will
disguise it. Double-sided adhesive tape
allows you to join paper invisibly. Matt
adhesive tape is more expensive than
ordinary adhesive tape, but it is much
less obvious on gift wraps.

Felt-tipped pens
Use felt-tipped pens rather than paint
for colouring photocopied gift wrap.

Florist's wire
This is very handy for tying on
decorations and for fastening loops of
ribbon when making big bows.

Saucers and glass sheets
Mix runny paints in saucers and spread
layers of thick paint on to glass for
potato and rubber stamp printing.

Glue
PVA (white) glue is a thick white liquid
that dries transparent. It will stick most
surfaces together in a reasonably short
drying time.

Hole punch
A multi-sized hole punch can be used
to decorate cards and make holes for
gift tags.

Paint
Use water-based paints such as acrylics,
poster paints or even sample pots of
household emulsion (latex) paint to
decorate your paper.

Paintbrushes
One broad and one fine-tipped
paintbrush will be useful for mixing
colours and painting striped papers.

Pattern wheel
A cheap dressmaker's tool that can be
used to make pierced patterns on card.

Hot glue gun
The glue gun delivers a small amount
of hot, melted glue at the squeeze of a
trigger. The glue dries almost instantly
and is very strong.

Rubber stamps
A huge selection of rubber stamps is
now available, and it only takes minutes

ABOVE *A selection of materials and
key equipment for creative stationery
and gift wrap.*

to stamp out coordinated gift wrap, tags
and cards.

Sealing wax
Drip the melted wax to make
decorative seals.

Small roller and tray
These are easy to use and ideal for
making up batches of matching paper.

Sponges
Sponges are great for printing your
own paper.

BEETLE STATIONERY

Hunt through nineteenth-century natural history books for engravings of weird and wonderful beetles, which you can use to decorate a matching set of greetings cards, envelopes, gift tags and postcards.

YOU WILL NEED

MATERIALS
thin card and writing paper in various colours and white
ready-made envelopes
photocopies of beetles
matt gold paper
glue stick
gold cord

EQUIPMENT
craft knife
ruler
cutting mat
scissors
hole punch

1 For postcards, use a craft knife and ruler to cut the coloured card to a suitable size. Measure your envelopes and cut the greetings cards to fit neatly inside when folded. Score down the centre with the blunt edge of the scissors. Use the scraps for gift tags and punch a single hole in the top.

2 Cut round the beetle motifs with the craft knife and ruler, making neat rectangles. Tear squares and rectangles of various sizes from the coloured card and gold paper.

3 Arrange the beetle shapes in a pleasing design on the paper or card. Glue each piece in place. Make sure the glue reaches right to the edges so that they don't curl up. Stick single motifs on the flaps of the envelopes and at the top of the writing paper. To complete the tags, thread a length of gold cord through each hole.

CUPID WRAPPING PAPER

This wrapping paper design, with its dropped-shadow image, can be achieved by stencilling or stamping. Home-made wrapping paper would be the perfect finishing touch for a Valentine's Day present or even for a Christmas present; choose colours to suit the occasion.

YOU WILL NEED

MATERIALS
cupid motif
acetate sheet
plain wrapping paper
acrylic paints: red oxide and gold

EQUIPMENT
black magic marker
craft knife
cutting mat
stencil brush
tile
paint roller
cupid rubber stamp

1 If you are using the stencil method, place a cupid motif (or a freehand sketch) under a sheet of acetate. Draw the image on the acetate with a magic marker. Cut it out with the craft knife to create the stencil.

2 Stencil the cupid on to the wrapping paper, using red oxide paint and a stencil brush. Allow to dry. Using gold paint, stencil the cupid slightly off-centre, to give a dropped-shadow effect.

3 If you are using the rubber stamp method, put some red oxide paint on to the tile and use the roller to coat the stamp. Stamp the images, then over-print using the stamp and the gold paint as before.

STARPRINT WRAPPING PAPER

Complete an original gift by dressing it up in original, hand-decorated wrapping paper. It's not only pretty, but fun to print. This star pattern printed in festive colours makes great Christmas wrapping.

YOU WILL NEED

MATERIALS
thin card
plain wrapping paper
water-based block printing
paints: red, green and white
water-based gold paint

EQUIPMENT
pair of compasses
pencil
scissors
white chalk
star-motif rubber stamp
paintbrush

1 Cut a circular template out of card and draw around it in chalk on the wrapping paper, spacing the circles evenly on the sheet.

2 Print alternate circles with red and green stars, brushing the paint evenly on the stamp between each print.

3 Print white stars in the middle of each circle, between the circles and in each of the corners.

4 Following the chalk circle between the stars, make rings of gold dots and dot the point of each star with A little gold.

GLORIOUS GIFT WRAP

If you want to make a gift extra special, why not design your own wrapping paper to suit the person to whom you are giving the present? Home-made gift wrap shows that you wanted to make your gift memorable.

YOU WILL NEED

MATERIALS
plain paper

EQUIPMENT
rubber stamps in a variety of motifs
stamp pads

1 To make a non-regimented design, first stamp on one edge of the paper. Then rotate the stamp in your hand to change the direction. Re-charge the stamp with ink as required.

2 Turn the paper and continue stamping the shapes. The end result should have roughly an even amount of background pattern.

3 To achieve a more formal pattern, begin by stamping a row of shapes along the bottom edge.

4 Build up the design, alternating between two colours if you like, to make an all-over pattern of closely spaced shapes.

SEAWEED GIFT WRAP

Swirling seaweed shapes in watery shades of green and blue, on a blue-green background, produce an underwater effect that makes a really unusual wrapping paper. Vary the colours of the paints depending on the colour of the background paper you choose.

YOU WILL NEED

MATERIALS
tracing paper
acetate sheet
blue-green wrapping paper
acrylic paints: sap-green, white
and blue

EQUIPMENT
pencil
fine black magic marker
craft knife
cutting mat
paint-mixing container
stencil brushes

1 Trace the template from the back of the book, enlarging if necessary. Go over the outline with the magic marker. Lay the acetate on top and carefully cut the stencil.

2 Position the stencil on the wrapping paper. Mix sap-green paint with a little white. Stencil motifs A and B side by side in rows across the paper, leaving space for a row of motif C between.

3 With white, add highlights to the seaweed tips.

4 Mix blue paint with white and stencil C in rows, leaving a stencil space in between for lighter coloured seaweed shapes.

EMBOSSED CARDS

Embossed paper has a subtle, expensive and specialist look about it, but it is in fact not at all difficult to make. Just follow the steps below.

YOU WILL NEED

MATERIALS
tracing paper
thin card
coloured paper, card and envelopes
PVA (white) glue
ribbon (optional)

EQUIPMENT
pencil
blunt and smooth-end plastic embossing tools
scissors
hole punch (optional)

1 Trace the templates from the back of the book, enlarging if necessary, and transfer to thin card. Cover it with the paper.

2 Holding down firmly, rub the paper gently over the cut-out area to define the shape. Increase the pressure until the shape shows up as a clear indentation. Turn the paper over.

3 Trim the paper shape and stick it to a card background. Pair it up with a contrasting envelope or punch a hole in it and thread a ribbon through to use as a gift tag.

WOODLAND GIFT WRAP

Look out for interestingly textured card and paper in complementary colours to make a whole range of greetings cards, postcards, gift wrap and gift tags for beautiful seasonal or birthday presents.

YOU WILL NEED

MATERIALS

tracing paper
thin card or paper
selection of coloured and
textured papers and card
corrugated paper
PVA (white) glue
stencil card
selection of acrylic paints
narrow paper ribbon
sealing wax
fresh leaves

EQUIPMENT

pencil
scissors
craft knife
cutting mat
brush
ruler
cotton wool or stencil brush
paint-mixing container
hole punch
safety matches

1 Trace the template from the back of the book, enlarging if necessary, and transfer to thin card or paper. Cut out. Cut a rectangle of coloured card and fold in half to make a greetings card. Draw around a leaf template on the front and cut out the shape. Cut a contrasting paper to the same size as the card and stick it on the inside.

2 Fold a second card, and draw around the template of the oak leaf on the reverse of the corrugated paper. Cut out the shape and glue it to the front of the card.

3 For the stencilled card, tear a square of coloured paper and glue it to the front of a piece of card. Draw around a leaf template on to stencil card and cut it out with a craft knife. Place the stencil on the coloured square and dab paint on to it with a ball of cotton wool or a stencil brush.

4 Use the same leaf stencil on a large sheet of coloured paper to make some co-ordinating gift wrap.

5 Make a selection of gift tags and postcards in the same way. Cut some leaf shapes out of coloured paper to make simple tags. Punch a hole in the tags and thread

6 Make your own simple envelopes by folding a piece of coloured paper to fit around a greetings card. Secure the flaps with melted sealing wax and decorate while it is still sticky with a small fresh leaf.

CELESTIAL WRAPPING PAPER

Red and gold suns grace a midnight-blue background to create wrapping paper that will be as special as the present you wrap in it. If you can't bear to part with the paper when you've finished making it, use it to cover a box such as a hatbox.

YOU WILL NEED

MATERIALS	EQUIPMENT
acrylic paints: gold and red	*2 plates*
white paper	*small paint roller*
acetate sheet	*sun-motif rubber stamp*
masking tape	*cutting mat*
plain blue wrapping paper	*craft knife*
newspaper	*stencil brush*

1 Put a little gold paint on a plate and roll the paint on to the stamp. Stamp a sun on the white paper. Put the paper on the cutting mat, place the acetate on top and secure with masking tape. Cut out the sun outline when dry with a craft knife. Place the stencil on the wrapping paper and secure with masking tape.

2 Put some red paint on another plate and dip in the stencil brush, dabbing off any excess on newspaper. Stipple the paint on the wrapping paper through the stencil. Repeat, moving the acetate and re-securing it, until the whole paper is covered in an orderly and spacious pattern of suns.

3 Put some more gold paint on the plate and roll the paint on to the stamp. Stamp the design on top of the red suns, as closely as possible to the original outline, to give a three-dimensional effect.

COLLAGE GIFT WRAP

Look along the racks of newspaper stands for interesting foreign scripts to incorporate in this special gift wrap. The newspaper is painted with translucent watercolour inks so that the print shows through.

YOU WILL NEED

MATERIALS

foreign language newspapers
watercolour inks
tracing paper
stencil card
white cartridge paper or coloured card
stencil paints: gold and black
corrugated card
plain gold gift wrap
glue stick

EQUIPMENT

pencil
paintbrush
craft knife
cellulose kitchen sponge
scissors

1 Paint sections of the newspaper in bright inks. Trace the template from the back of the book, enlarging if necessary, and transfer to stencil card. Cut out.

2 Paint cartridge paper in different coloured inks or use coloured card. Stencil the paper in black and gold.

3 Cut a Christmas tree from sponge and stick it to a piece of corrugated card. Stamp some of the coloured newsprint with gold trees.

4 Tear strips, rectangles and tree shapes from the newsprint. Tear around the stamped and stencilled motifs and cut out some with scissors. Glue in place on the gift wrap.

FLOWER-STENCILLED WRAP

If you have taken trouble to find a really special gift, home-made wrapping paper is the perfect finishing touch. Once the stencil is cut, this design doesn't take long to do and its effect is truly magnificent.

YOU WILL NEED

MATERIALS
tracing paper
acetate sheet
green crepe paper
acrylic or stencil paints: raw umber, white and yellow

EQUIPMENT
pencil
indelible black magic marker
craft knife
cutting mat
paint-mixing container
stencil brush

1 Trace the template from the back of the book, enlarging if necessary, and transfer to the acetate sheet. The design is made from two pieces: the petals and the centre. Cut each part out separately.

2 Using the flower centre stencil, apply raw umber paint to the crepe paper. Position the stencil at random, covering the paper; be sure to allow enough room between the centres for the petals.

3 Lighten the raw umber with white paint, and apply as a highlight.

4 Take the second stencil and, taking care to align it properly over the first, stencil the petals in yellow.

ROMANTIC GIFT WRAP

What better way to present the perfect Valentine's Day gift than wrapped in this hand-stencilled paper with bold hearts? This is an easy stencil to cut out and use. Your finishing touch won't take you long to complete, and you are sure to end up with a really professional result.

1 Drawing a heart freehand onto a sheet of acetate sheet. Carefully cut out the design.

2 Stencil burnt umber hearts randomly across the paper. Allow to dry.

3 Stencil gold hearts on top and slightly to the right. The umber hearts should look like the gold heart's shadows.

YOU WILL NEED

MATERIALS
*tracing paper
acetate sheet
crepe paper
acrylic paints: burnt umber
and gold*

EQUIPMENT
*pencil
indelible black magic marker
craft knife
cutting mat
stencil brush
paint-mixing container*

PRIVATE CORRESPONDENCE

This personalized stationery makes a statement before you even put pen to paper. Although there are many ways of making stationery using pre-cut rubber stamps, this project goes one step further and shows you how to make your own rubber stamp from an eraser. Choose images that express something about your character.

YOU WILL NEED

MATERIALS
*drawings of chosen motif
plain paper
new eraser
liquid lighter fuel
embossing ink and powder
(optional)*

EQUIPMENT
*craft knife
cutting mat
lino-cutting tool
stamp pad*

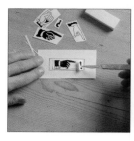

1 Cut out and arrange your motifs on a piece of paper so they will fit on to the eraser.

2 Photocopy the motif arrangement and cut out the shape to fit the eraser.

3 Place this squarely on the eraser, with the drawing face down.

4 Spread about three drops of liquid lighter fuel over the back of the paper. Make sure that the paper does not slide across the eraser as you do this.

5 Remove the paper to reveal the transferred design. This will be reversed, but the stamping process will reverse it again, bringing it back to the original image.

6 Use a fine lino-cutting tool and a craft knife to cut around the outline and the pattern details. Scoop out any excess to leave the design standing proud of the eraser.

7 Press the eraser stamp into a coloured stamp pad and print your stationery. For a raised image, stamp the motif with some embossing ink and then sprinkle with embossing powder.

BUTTERFLY GIFT WRAP

Original, hand-printed wrapping paper can make an ordinary present into something very special.

YOU WILL NEED

MATERIALS
tracing paper
acetate sheet
coloured paper
masking tape
acrylic paints: red and black

EQUIPMENT
pencil
indelible black magic marker
craft knife
cutting mat
stiff brush

1 Trace the template from the back of the book, enlarging if necessary. Place a piece of acetate over it and use a magic marker to draw the wings for the first stencil. Use a second piece of acetate to make a second stencil of the body and the wing markings.

2 Cut out both stencils. Secure the first stencil lightly to the paper with masking tape and stipple on the red paint. Do not overload the brush. Reposition the acetate and repeat to cover the paper.

3 When the red paint is dry, secure the second stencil in place with masking tape. Stipple on the black paint and repeat the process to complete the butterflies.

VALENTINE'S CARD

Hand-made cards really do convey your feelings. This special card captures the spirit of some elaborate Victorian Valentine's cards, with its combination of gold and silver lace, soft, velvety pink background and central cupid motif.

YOU WILL NEED

MATERIALS
*paper glue
dark pink paper,
15 x 15 cm/6 x 6 in
gold card,
20 x 20 cm/8 x 8 in
decorative gold cake band
silver, white and gold
paper doilies
lilac and dark green
paper scraps
Victorian-style cupid motif*

EQUIPMENT
scissors

1 Glue the pink paper to the gold card, leaving an equal margin all around. Trim the edges with narrow strips of gold foil lace, cut from the cake band. Cut out a small silver flower for each corner from the silver doilies.

2 Cut out four white petals and two flower shapes from a white doily and back them with lilac paper. Choose a larger rectangular shape for the centre and back it with green paper. Stick the shapes on to the background.

3 Cut out silver flowers and white leaves and glue them around the edges of the main shape, in an interesting pattern.

4 Finish by fixing the cupid to the centre and adding more cut-out gold flowers.

TAURUS GIFT WRAP

Personalize a gift by creating some of this original gift wrap that is stencilled with the appropriate star-sign. Strong dark red and black have been used here to match the energetic, earthy character of the Taurean. Don't overfill the brush when stencilling: blot any excess paint on paper towels before you begin. If paint does seep under the edges of the stencil, wipe it away carefully before repositioning the acetate.

YOU WILL NEED

MATERIALS
*thin card or paper
acetate sheet
plain deep red gift wrap
masking tape
black acrylic paint*

EQUIPMENT
*pencil
black magic marker
craft knife
cutting mat
stencil brush
paper towels*

1 Draw a template following the finished picture above on card or paper. Place the acetate over the template and trace the outline with a magic marker.

2 Carefully cut out the stencil using a craft knife.

3 Decide on the positioning of the motifs on the paper, marking lightly with a pencil if necessary. Position the stencil and use a little masking tape to hold it in place. Stipple the design with the stencil brush. Lift the stencil off carefully and repeat to cover the paper.

ROSE-STAMPED STATIONERY

Hand-printed stationery sends its own message, even before you have added your greetings or invitation. This golden rose would be particularly suitable for wedding stationery, making a welcome change from the usual mass-produced cards.

YOU WILL NEED

MATERIALS
tracing paper
lino square
gold paint
blank stationery, such as
deckle-edged notepaper and
envelopes
stationery box
Japanese paper, cut into strips
glue stick
ribbon

EQUIPMENT
pencil
lino-cutting tools
cutting mat
small paint roller
paper towels
fine paintbrush

1 Trace the template from the back of the book, and transfer to lino. Using a narrow-grooved tool, cut out the motif, keeping your free hand behind the blade at all times. With a wide tool, cut away the excess lino. Indicate with an arrow which edge is the top, on the back.

2 Ink the lino stamp with gold paint and stamp the stationery, re-inking the roller each time. Wipe away any build-up of paint with paper towels.

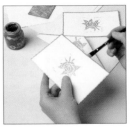

3 Edge the envelopes, cards and the top edge of the notepaper with a fine line of gold paint. Glue the box with strips of Japanese paper. Arrange the notepaper and cards in the box. Bind the envelopes with more Japanese paper and ribbon and add them to the box. Decorate the box lid with a pretty ribbon.

CONTEMPLATIVE CUPID CARD

This elaborate hand-made card isn't difficult to make and will tell someone special that they are in your thoughts. Some ordinary pencils are water-soluble, so try what you have before buying pencils specially!

YOU WILL NEED

MATERIALS

tracing paper
masking tape
heavy watercolour paper
thin card
water-soluble pencils:
dark and light green, dark and light blue, red, pink and grey
watercolour or drawing inks:
pink and orange
all-purpose glue
glitter glue

EQUIPMENT

pencil
cutting mat
craft knife
scissors
fine paintbrush
heavy book

1 Trace the templates from the back of the book, enlarging if necessary. Tape the background and cupid tracings to the watercolour paper and go over the outlines with a pencil, leaving an indentation on the paper. Fold along the fold lines.

2 Transfer the design for the frame to the thin card in the same way. Cut out the card and frame and fold them.

3 Colour in the background and cupid, using water-soluble pencils, and cut out the cupid. On spare pieces of watercolour paper, draw and colour in some simple flowers and stems. Go over the pencil work with a wet paintbrush to blend the colours.

4 Decorate the outside of the card with watercolour or drawing ink, mixing the colours for a patchy effect.

5 Cut out the flowers, stick them together and apply a little glitter glue on to the centres. Apply glitter glue to the wings of the cupid.

6 Line up the edges of the cupid with the edges of the background at points A and C. Stick on some flowers.

7 Stick the frame to the front of the card at point D. Attach a few more flowers to the inside of the frame. Outline the leaves.

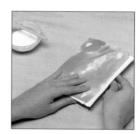

8 Finally, stick the background and cupid into the card, taking care to line up points B. Stick flap A to join the card together and fold up the card. Press it under a book before sending.

ROLLER PLAIDS

This project borrows materials from the home decorator, using two paint rollers with emulsion (latex) paint to form the basic checkered pattern. The plaid effect is added in two stages, with drying time in between.

YOU WILL NEED

MATERIALS
terracotta-pink emulsion
(latex) paint
white paper
olive-green watercolour paint
white acrylic, poster or
gouache paint
adhesive tape
red string

EQUIPMENT
small paint roller, with integral
paint tray
2 saucers
square-tipped and fine
paintbrushes
scissors

1 Put pink paint in the tray and coat the roller. Begin just in from the edge and run parallel stripes down the length of the paper.

2 Allow to dry, then do the same horizontally. Leave to dry thoroughly.

3 Put the olive-green paint in a saucer and paint stripes on the paper that cross through the centres of the white squares.

4 Dilute the white paint in a saucer and paint fine lines that cross through the centres of the solid pink squares.

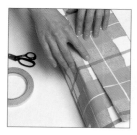

5 Place your gift on the paper and wrap it carefully.

6 Wrap the red string around the gift and tie it in a knot at the centre. Unravel the individual threads of the string to make a crinkly bow.

LEO LETTER RACK

This jolly letter rack is just the thing to brighten up your desk.

YOU WILL NEED

MATERIALS
5 mm/¼ in birch plywood sheet, cut as follows:
base 21.5 x 7.3 cm/
8½ x 2⅞ in
sides 13 x 7.3 cm/5 x 2⅞ in
front 23 x 10 cm/9 x 4 in
back 23 x 19 cm/9 x 7½ in
tracing paper
wood glue
masking tape
4 wooden balls, 15 mm/⅝ in
white undercoat paint
acrylic paints: deep cobalt,
deep yellow, cadmium-red,
gold, raw umber and black
matt varnish

EQUIPMENT
pencil & ruler
pair of compasses
fretsaw
sandpaper
paintbrushes
stencil brush

1 Mark out the back, front, base and two sides on the plywood to the sizes listed above. Trace the template from the back of the book, enlarging if necessary, and cut out the back and sides. Cut out the other pieces. Sand the edges.

2 Glue the pieces together and hold in place with tape until the glue has hardened completely. Remove the tape and sand all the edges and corners. Glue the wooden balls to the corners of the base.

3 Paint the letter rack with white undercoat, sanding down lightly when dry. With the stencil brush, stipple the rack with deep cobalt paint.

4 Complete the design in acrylic paints, using the main picture as a guide. Seal with a coat of matt varnish.

STARRY LETTER RACK

Painted in a lovely midnight-blue with jolly yellow stars, this charming letter rack is quite straightforward to assemble.

YOU WILL NEED

MATERIALS	EQUIPMENT
tracing paper	*pencil*
5 mm / ¼ in birch plywood	*ruler*
sheet	*pair of compasses*
wood glue	*fretsaw*
masking tape	*sandpaper*
4 wooden balls, 15 mm / ⅝ in	*paintbrushes*
white undercoat paint	
acrylic paints	
satin varnish	

1 Trace the template from the back of the book, enlarging as required. Mark on the plywood, then cut out and sand all the edges.

2 Glue the pieces together and hold in place with masking tape until the glue has hardened completely.

3 Remove the tape and sand all the edges and corners. Glue the wooden balls to the corners of the base.

4 Paint on a coat of white undercoat, sanding down lightly when dry. Paint the rack and the stars in acrylic paints. Seal with a coat of satin varnish. When the varnish is completely dry, glue the stars in position on the front of the rack.

STAR TREE ORNAMENT

You can buy pre-cut polystyrene shapes from craft suppliers, and these little stars are ideal for dressing up to go on the Christmas tree. Multi-coloured sequins and tiny beads turn them into exotic treasures. Attach the sequins along the points of the stars or cover the whole surface for an extravagant effect.

YOU WILL NEED

MATERIALS
*polystyrene star shape,
about 8 cm/3 in across
gold spray paint
small piece of plasticine
multi-coloured glass
seed and seed pearl beads
multi-coloured sequins
special design sequins
1.5 cm/½ in brass-headed pins
small containers
thin gold braid*

1 Spray the polystyrene shape gold, anchoring it with a piece of plasticine to stop it blowing away when spraying. Allow to dry.

2 Sort the beads, sequins and pins into different containers to make it easier to choose your colours and shapes as you work.

3 Thread a seed bead on to a pin, followed by a sequin. Push into the polystyrene. Repeat to complete the design. In the centre of each side of the star, pin a seed pearl and a cup sequin or other special design.

4 Attach a small loop of thin gold braid to hang the ornament from the tree.

XMAS TREE GIFT TAGS

Spend some time making yourself a selection of stamped, stencilled and painted motifs before you begin to assemble these gift tags.

YOU WILL NEED

MATERIALS	EQUIPMENT
tracing paper	*pencil*
thin card	*scissors*
cellulose kitchen sponge	*paintbrush*
corrugated card	*hole punch*
glue stick	
coloured and textured papers	
stencil card	
stencil paints: black and gold	
white cartridge paper	
watercolour inks	
white oil crayon	
brown parcel wrap	
gift tags	
hole punch	
fine gold cord	

1 Trace the template from the back of the book, enlarging if necessary, transfer to paper and cut out. Draw around the template on sponge and cut out so you have a positive and a negative image to use as stamps. Glue each stamp on card. Stamp both motifs in gold on to a selection of papers.

2 Trace the branch pattern and transfer it to a stencil card. Cut out and stencil in black and gold on to a selection of papers and on some of the stamped motifs.

3 Paint cartridge paper in bright inks and cut out a star motif. Scribble spots on parcel wrap with a white oil crayon to make snowflakes. Tear them out individually, leaving a small border.

4 Assemble the tags. Cut or tear out a selection of motifs and arrange them on the cards. Glue in place. Punch a hole in the top and thread each with a loop of fine cord.

Papier-mâché Mirror, p14

Seashell Mirror, p15

Folk Art Frames, p19

Coronet Picture Frame, p24

King of Hearts Mirror, p36

Wooden Star Frame, p38

Pinpricked Lampshade, p48

Stencilled Roller Blind, p55

Painted Chair, p56

Sponge-printed
Shelf, p68

Wastepaper Bin, p67

Yellow Roses
Lampshade, p69

Ivy Stool, p70

Stippled Storage Tins, p59

Fruity Bracelet, p85

Winged Cupid Brooch, p88

Shooting Star Badge, p97

Sun and Moon Badges, p95

Moulded Earrings, p110

Embroidered Jewellery, p98

Jewellery Pouch, p106

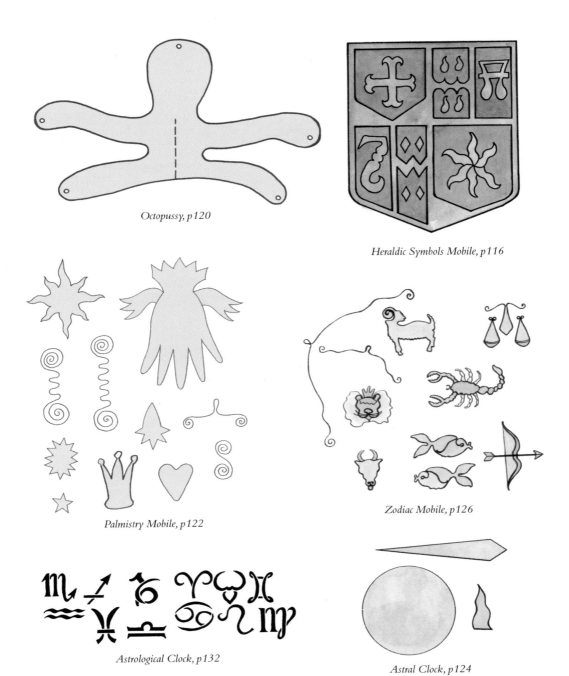

Octopussy, p120

Heraldic Symbols Mobile, p116

Palmistry Mobile, p122

Zodiac Mobile, p126

Astrological Clock, p132

Astral Clock, p124

Wire Sunflower Mobile, p138

Sea Creatures Mobile, p134

Tex Mex Clock, p140

Celestial Mobile, p141

Papier-mâché Mobile, p144

Sunburst Clock, p142

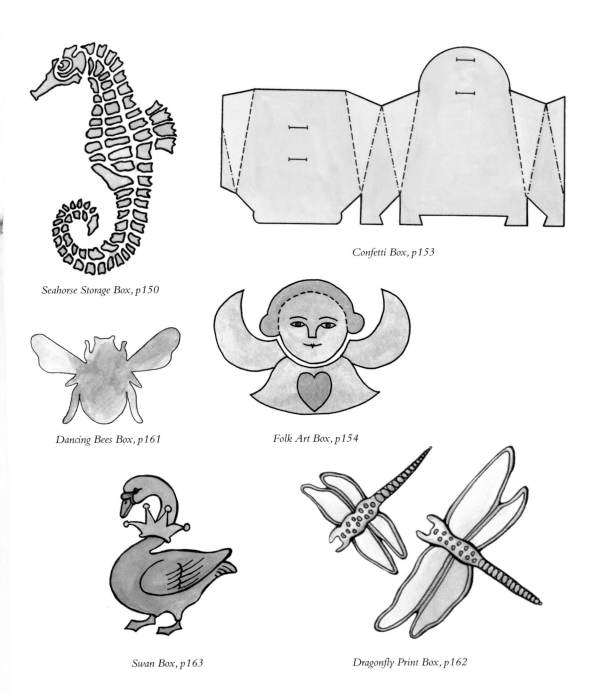

Seahorse Storage Box, p150

Confetti Box, p153

Dancing Bees Box, p161

Folk Art Box, p154

Swan Box, p163

Dragonfly Print Box, p162

Cancer Crab Box, p167

Busy Bee Workbox, p168

Fleur-de-lys Box, p170

Painted Sewing Box, p176

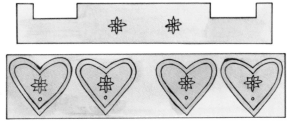

Hand-painted Box, p178

English Lion Cushion, p184

Stencilled Tablecloth, p186

Fruity Appliqué Cushion, p188

Astrological Cushion, p191

*Muslin (Cheesecloth)
Curtain, p190*

Shelf Edging, p206

Sea Pillowcase, p194

Scented Cushion, p195

Silk-painted Curtain, p196

Peg Bag, p200

Nursery Cushion, p198

Quilted Cushion, p201

Needlepoint Cushion, p203

Cushion with Seashells, p204

Painted Tablecloth, p202

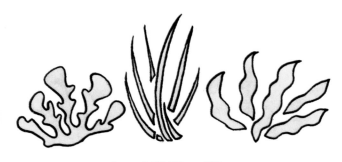

Seaweed Gift Wrap, p222

Embossed Cards, p223

Woodland Gift Wrap, p224

Collage Gift Wrap, p227
Xmas Tree Gift Tags, p243

Flower-stencilled Wrap, p228

Butterfly Gift Wrap, p232

Rose-stamped Stationery, p235

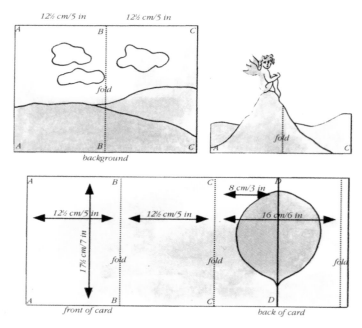

background

Contemplative Cupid Card, p236

Leo Letter Rack, p240

Starry Letter Rack, p241

INDEX

ACKNOWLEDGEMENTS

The publishers would like to thank the following for their invaluable contribution to this volume:

Projects Ofer Acoo, Madeleine Adams, Dinah Alan-Smith, Deborah Alexander, Evelyn Bennett, Amanda Blunden, Petra Boase, Penny Boylan, Janet Bridge, Louise Brownlow, Esther Burt, Judy Clayton, Gill Clement, Lilli Curtiss, Sophie Embleton, Lucinda Ganderton, Louise Gardam, Lisa Gilchrist, Andrew Gilmore, Dawn Gulyas, David Hancock, Jill Hancock, Stephanie Harvey, Bridget Hinge, Labeena Ishaque, Sameena Ishaque, Mary Maguire, Rachel Howard Marshall, Abigail Mill, Terence Moore, Izzy Moreau, Jack Moxley, Oliver Moxley, Cleo Mussie, Sarbjitt Natt, Cheryl Owen, Emma Petitt, Lizzie Reakes, Kim Rowley, Deborah Schneebeli-Morrell, Debbie Siniska, Isabel Stanley, Adele Tipler, Kellie-Marie Townsend, Karen Triffitt, Liz Wagstaff, Sally Walton, Stewart Walton, Emma Whitfield, Josephine Whitfield, Melanie Williams and Dorothy Wood
Photography Steve Dalton, James Duncan, Michelle Garrett, Lucy Mason, Gloria Nicol, Debbie Patterson and Peter Williams

Caerleon 12.6.15